S.

Trocchio · Ceruaro · Pedecone · Venafre · Capria · Lo Gallo · Scapito · Boiano · Vinchiatura

S. Vettore · Nuntiata à luga · Tercina · Fossa Cecca · R. Minolfa

Vadro · S. Pietro infra · R. Pipirozza · Curlano · Voltumo f. · Lotino · Le Fere · S. Polo · La Gardia

S. Maria · m. Ritodo · Pratella · Loscie · S.G.

Migliano · Cesina · Mastrate · Prata · Laualle · Il Capraro · Supino · Altilia

Camini · Calaurito · Pianola · Lepentime · R. Vecchia · Limagna · Bosco S. · Mutri · Cassinoro

Cocurueo · Priello · Presenzano · Ailano · Curti · Siluestro · Capo di Capo · Callearso

Mortula · Leuagli · Serola · Lopatio · S. Gregorio · Mutri

Cuntugni · S. Clementi · Tora · La Ferrara · Il Castello · S. Croce

Sepiciano · S. Croce · Catagli · Marcian · S. Felice · S. Polito · Caio · Petra Roia

Palifisco · S. Mar · R. Mofena · S. M. della cor- · Petra · Vaia · Sepiciano · Colle di Mezzo · Cosauo · Cintella

S. Cilio · tino · Garofali · Marzano · dee · Vaiarano · Caluisi · Il Monaco · La Corti

S. Antonio · Rocolifi · Tarrano · Carbonaro · Paternole host · Strauighano · Cosino · Carrettaò · Facelli · Massa · Cerrito

Lauro · Fontana Ra- · Torre · Casafredda · Auersano · Riardo · R. Romani · Trocorse · Selua · Pughianello · m. Aerro · R. di casale

Piano · dina · Cosale · Petra Mo- · Li Proffetti · S. Samegne · de alifi · Telefo · Veroli

di Seßa · Sessa · Ligusti · Tiamo · lara · Schiaui · Selua · Casale · S. Agatella · Lima ta · S. M.

Sorniello · Lascano · Casale · Montanaro · M. Mauri · Mairano · Piaua · Campagnano

Lo Carno · Ventorulio · La ricchielta · La Croce · Villa · Trebbia · Roiano · Aluigna · nello

Pie di monte Carmola · Nocelleto · T. di Francolifi · Fonera · Aluignano · Le Serola · Licafari · Solopauo

Quintola · S. Bartolome · Toricello · Iano · Foiento · Pontelatroue · S. M.

M. Massice · S. Croce · Limarisco · Calui · Formicola · Stragolagalora · Aluigna · della grotta

R. M. dragone · L'oliuetto · S. Aniello · Pignataro · Palôbara · Caiazzo · Campagnano

Bagni · Falciano · Limara · Sparanisi · Romagnano · Vitolasio · Cefarano · Li Torielli · Torr

S. Angelo · Ceparlo · S. Anastasia · Lo Pizzone · S. Andrea · Vellona · S. M. Hierusalê · Squilli · Melizzano · Cacciano

Torre · Bertolet · Brezze · S. Chiumêto · T. Refisco · Auirano · Oucenta · S. Pietr

Cacello · S. M. della fossa · Capua · Limatoia · Frascio · Tocco · Pr

Voltumo f. · Arnone · Grazzanifi · S. Mauro · S. Nicola · Morrone

C. del Voltorno · Mazzono · Cauallarizza · Caferta · Biruo · Fagnaro · Tauurno

Clanio, ouero Patria f. · S. Andrea · S. Prisco · Aregano · Laualle fusana · S. Maria · M. Sachia

Vena · P. a. Selice · T. di Caseria · Bagnoli · S. Agata · Aerola

Padula · Casal di Precise · Casaluce · Macerata · Rechele · Durazzano · S. Martino

Archerusia · Vico di · Frogano Piccolo · Aprano · Loriano · S. Chimento · Forchia · Vorano · Valli

Pantano · Fregnano · Casolla · Teuerola · Marcianifi · Metaloni · Ritodi · Loffr

Lago · Il Gaudo · maiore · Cefa · Casa Poze- · Tretola · S. Felice · Uncino · Pantanaru

di Patria · Pozzo Spararo · Anersa · Soccia · na · Ulmo, cupo · Cancello · Aricio · Paulifi · Bad

Pozzo nuouo · Parete · Orta · Pescarnola · Talanico · Ceruaara

Patria · Fugliano · S. Arpino · Pomigliano · S. Archagelo · Cauano · Sessela · Il Castello · Orcino · Ottofaghi · Il Pizone

Zaccarina · Panicocolo · S. Antano · Frattam · Cella · Cerra · Gaudello · Fellin

Barcaturo · Mognano · Grumi · Fratta maggiore · Acerra · Anella

Marano · Cassadrò · Cardito · Casale nuouo · Ponticello · Larocca

Li Coli · Beluedere · Chiaiano · Crispano · Fraolo · Pomigladarco · Bruciano · Marcigliano · Nola · Sporone · Magn.

Nacaretti · Casriola · Casoria · Pomigliano · Vanano · Cardinaro

Cuma · M. Riscello · Liquarte · Ilgaudo · Puluica · Arpino · Il Salice · S. Vittaghano · Cimitno · Cecala · Casamaciano

S. Martino · Fusara · Soccaua · C.S. Ermo · S. Galiano · S. Vito · Sirico · Serino

Auerno · Udo a' Sto · Attignano · Scifeiano · Palazzo · Montaro

Baia · Pozzuolo · Agnano · Napoli · Poggio reale · Anaftasie · S. Paolo · Cast

T. di Fume · Foregrotte · S. Leonardo · Ponticella · Pollena · Sautano · Lauruno

S. M. Pie di grotte · Lo Casale · Massa · Serino · Trocchia · Ottaiano · Migliano

La Scroffa · Abolla gra- · S. Gio atten- · La barra · S. Sebastiano · Palma · Aruara

Ischia · ta · Nisita · tia · Menzohno · duci · S. Jorio · Portici · M. Vefuuio · Lauri · Casola

Schiaia Romana · Mare Morto · S. Stratto · Golfo · Refina · Termine bianco

Laura · Procita · Capo di Miseno · Lagaola · C. di Posilipo · di · Edella fico · Lemarine · S. M. della foce

L. Apparato · Napoli · Gl. in Curabili · S. M.ª Iacona Striano · Sarno

T. del Greco · S. Angelo · Tre Case · S. Martino

T. ripa Stretta · T.P. Ancino · S. Pietro · Braccuglia

Scafata · Valli

T. dell Aunuciata

PASQUALINA'S TABLE

The table is where all the magic happens...

PASQUALINA'S TABLE

Our Italian Family Traditions
...The Gluten-Free Way

Book Design, Photographs and Illustrations
By Carmine Raspaolo

Copyright

Acknowledgments:

The making of *"Pasqualina's Table"* brings us back in time to our family history, stories, and traditions. The table is where all the magic happens - laughter, joy, crying, celebrations, and simple togetherness. It's where stories, family, love and friendships are honored. "Tutti a tavola" (everyone at the table) is popular for a reason! It's where life unfolds, coupled with beautiful and delicious traditional foods and drinks.

Recreating these special recipes was a fun and complicated process that required the efforts of my sister Lucia, my brother Carmine, and my mamma, Giovanna, without whom this book would not have been possible. Thank you for your continued support, confidence, enthusiasm, guidance and many laughs. Thank you for being honest taste testers, never being afraid to tell me when a gluten-free alternative had to be refined. I am extremely grateful to them and to my family and friends in Italy and the United States who were always available to answer any question and offer fantastic advice. To my super talented sister Lucia for taking the time to go to various markets with me and spending many days and nights in the kitchen recreating our family recipes into gluten-free versions with so much patience, attention and love for detail. To my brother Carmine, who never complained and was always present unpacking and repacking his video and camera equipment, taking beautiful photographs, videotaping, coaching and for his incredible work in capturing the love and passion of our family traditions. To my mamma Giovanna, for sharing so many wonderful family stories and her own delectable recipes, all of which stem from her memory and emotions, even if some of what she shared was difficult to translate. Finally, I am indebted to my dear friend and personal editor, Roseann Cigna, for her friendship and her brilliance and for dedicating many hours looking at my notes, editing and polishing my writing.

To the loves of my life:

My great nephews and nieces:
Miles, Kelly, Dashiell, Patrick and Maeve
for all the love, joy and happiness
they bring into our hearts.
May they continue to carry out our
family traditions that keep
us bonded together.

Table of Contents

Our Story x

Introduction xii

The Neapolitan Proverbs xiii

Rustic Neapolitan Appetizers 3
Fried Mini Pizzas 4
Potato Croquettes 6
Twice Baked Bread with Beans 8

Salads 11
Cod Salad 12
Reinforcement Salad 14

Soups of the Campania Region 17
Lentil Soup 18
Corn Pizza, Beans, and Vegetable Soup 20
The Wedding Soup 22

Pasta, Pizza, and Sauces 25
Escarole Pie 26
Genovese Sauce 28
Macaroni Frittata 30
Meat Based Tomato Sauce 32
Pasta, Potatoes, and Provola 34
Pasta and Beans 36

From The Oven 41
Potato Gateau (Casserole) 42
Mamma's Stuffed Peppers 44
Zucchini Parmigiana 46
Baked Tagliatelle Birds Nests 48

Table of Contents (continued)

Meat Dishes 53

Goat with Peas, Cacio and Eggs 54

Mamma's Meatballs 56

Mamma's Roasted Lamb with Potatoes 58

Pork with Potatoes and Papacelle 60

Sausage and Friarielli 62

Fish Dishes 65

Peppered Mussels 66

Poached Octopus 68

Seafood Risotto 70

Vegetables 73

Friggitelli Peppers with Tomatoes 74

Grilled Artichokes 76

Scapece Style Zucchini 78

Desserts and Snacks 81

Anise Taralli 82

Easter Pie 84

Ricotta Cheesecake 88

Walnut cups 90

What is Gluten? 92

Gluten-Free Flours & Starches 93

Gluten-Free Binders & Leaveners 97

Gluten -Free Flour Blends & Mixes 98

Glossary of Kitchen Utensils 99

Index 104

"Why do you do what you do?" This is a great question I am often asked and one that is simple to respond to. My "Why" has always been and will forever be "My Family." I once read a quote that stated, "People come into your life for a reason, a season, or lifetime." It's so true and some people become part of the family. Family is not only about being related by blood. It's about people in our lives that express true love, honesty, loyalty and respect for one another that makes us family. Those who know me recognize how passionate I am about family and traditions.

Italian food is an essential element of the "Italian experience" for its ability to represent the country and its culture, for its international recognition, attractiveness and deliciousness, and for its incredible ability to generate sharing and storytelling. The culinary arts and traditions have always been a big part of my life and one that I took for granted in the past. Instead of looking at the culinary arts as a career path for me, I embarked on an exciting journey, where most of my time and money was spent on education and on jobs that were interesting but not particularly fulfilling. Don't get me wrong. I'm so very grateful for these life experiences because on this journey of life, I've met some incredibly passionate and wonderful people with whom I have established strong and enduring friendships. I can't imagine life without them. Yet, with all of my education and experiences, here I am back to my roots and back to food and traditions. Food has always been an integral part of Italian culture and often is the main topic of conversation because food goes beyond simple nourishment.

Growing up as an Italian immigrant, I learned to value family, food, and faith from an early age. Cultural and culinary traditions are kept alive as my family cooks like they did in Italy with an array of authentic dishes passed from one generation to the next. Our unique and strong ties keep us together. It's our way of life where every element of the family culture is permeated by food, faith, family, music, gardening, and simply living the Italian way. It's a way of life that is cherished and never lost.

In 1973, my family and I moved from Naples, Italy to New York City on a ship called *"The Michelangelo"* (yes, I am literally "off the boat") where we lived with extended family that had emigrated from Italy years before. Traditional foods were prepared throughout the day, most of which originated from the towns of Campania, primarily the commune of Benevento and Napoli (Naples), the regional capital and the city where I was born. My family still maintains such traditions as making their own pasta, bread, wine, and tomato sauce. Nothing brings more joy to an Italian home than traditional food influenced by the old country and its heritage.

*The Michelangelo
Moving from Naples, Italy
Arriving in New York City 1973*

Nonna Gianna, My Mamma, at 18 years of age

My journey to become a chef began a few years ago after several family members developed autoimmune diseases and could no longer eat foods containing gluten. In order for them to enjoy family traditions, I began my quest by taking my mamma's traditional baking recipes and transforming them into delicious gluten-free alternatives. Many hours have been spent testing and refining our methods. Nonna Gianna's Gluten-Free baking was born at Culinary Genes and quickly became a hit amongst our family and friends. I named it Nonna Gianna's Traditions in honor of my mamma Giovanna, the most talented and amazing baker I know!

For the first time ever during Easter of 2020, our family could not be together in person. Thus the idea for this book was born during

Holy Week. It was then that we created the "Family QuaranTeam" and the development of gluten-free traditional family recipes to share with family and friends. While many of these recipes were developed and served during various holiday seasons, these are meals that you can prepare for a special day, family time, or simply when you feel like cooking food that comforts your soul. The kitchen is where you can spend time with people you love, creating and cooking together.

Easter or "Pasqua" in Italian has always been one of my favorite holidays for so many different reasons - the colors, the festivities, the gathering of family and friends, and the traditions. Pasqualina means "a child of Easter" and I was named after my Grandmother, the individual where most of these recipes emanate from. I decided to share with you 33 (thirty-three) of my family favorites and recreate them to gluten-free alternatives so that those with gluten-free intolerance or sensitivity can enjoy these delicacies as well. Because this book was created during Easter, I decided on "33" recipes for two reasons: (1) "33" was Jesus' age when he was crucified and resurrected, which gives us a meaning of renewed hope and a new beginning; (2) "33" symbolizes a high degree of spiritual consciousness that resonates with inspiration, courage, compassion, and honesty.

These delectable dishes were created by memory and emotions because nothing was ever written down in Italy so recipes did not exist. Instead, I followed family members in the United States and Italy with pen and paper to develop recipes that are clear on both ingredients and measurements. This was an exceptionally challenging but entertaining task! Their measurements usually consisted of "a little bit of this and a little bit of that." Right! So how do we convert "a little bit of this and a little bit of that" into understandable units of measurement? It continues to be an enlightening experience for which I am incredibly grateful. These recipes were made with love and stem from a commitment to keep my family's recipes and traditions alive, the gluten-free way. I leave you with some of my favorite dishes, which have been passed down and enjoyed for centuries. I am excited to share them and may they bring you and your family the same joy as they have in mine.

Tutti a Tavola e Buon Appetito! (Everyone to the table and Enjoy your meal!)

Lucia and Carmine
My Sister and Brother
at the beach in Naples, 1964

Pasqualina and Rocco
My Grandparents, Durazzano 1950s

My Family
1965

Introduction

Food is one of the greatest pleasures and a fundamental component of life. Eating gives an unparalleled sense of happiness, especially in Campania Italy, a region so rich in the culinary world and known for its ancient ruins and striking coastlines along the Tyrrhenian Sea. This love of food makes Campania the fascinating region that it is!

In Campania the development of regional cuisine is due to the inspiration and experience of the inhabitants of the area, who have skillfully turned the ingredients that were once considered to be typical peasant food into masterpieces. Campania is known as the land of the sun, the sea and culture. The simplicity of flavors and wholesome ingredients are the strengths of the typical dishes of this region. Campania cuisine also has the undisputed merit of having contributed to the birth and spread of the well-known Mediterranean diet, due to the use of products such as olive oil, vegetables, fruits and seafood. My family's traditional recipes are based on what they grew up with. In spite of the region's poverty, there has always been enthusiasm for food throughout the centuries. Foods were largely based on pasta and vegetables grown in their gardens, along with milk from sheep, cows and goats used to make cheese.

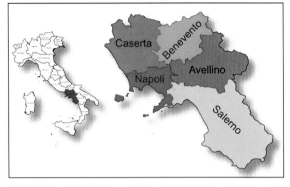

The provinces of Campania are: Naples (the regional capital), Caserta, Benevento, Avellino, and Salerno, including islands in the Gulf of Naples, Ischia, Procida, and Capri - true natural wonders.

When living in Naples, I remember visiting my grandparents on weekends in a mountain town called Durazzano, a municipality in the province of Benevento, the town where my mamma was born. On one of those weekends my grandmother and I went to pick up milk from a local farmer. She handed me a vintage aluminum cup, almost like a small bucket with a handle, and off we went. When we reached the farm, I handed the farmer the cup and he filled it with fresh milk directly from the cow, which was always warm and creamy. I noticed that he always had a large pail under the cow and milked the cow from the side, which led to several questions running through my mind. We were both intrigued because I was fascinated by the entire process and he was fascinated that I was genuinely interested in knowing and understanding the secrets of milking a cow by hand. Much to my surprise the farmer decided to give me the chance to experience this deep-rooted agricultural tradition that our ancestors made appear so effortless. After a brief lesson on how to properly milk the cow, I asked if the cow gets mad when you milk it. After a chuckle, he explained that the cow was milked from the side because it was safer and kept the tail out of the milk pail and his face. It also made it harder for the cow to kick the farmer. I sat on the farmers stool, which was made out of a large tree trunk, contemplating his last statement. Feeling a little intimidated I began my first milking as directed and not even a trickle came out. I continued to try and was getting frustrated, which only made my first experience at milking unpleasant. I could not get the right movement. Maybe it was because I was only 6 years old and quite honestly, I worried that the cow was going to kick me! We switched places so that the farmer could show me again and there it was, the milk easily flowed out into the pail. I tried again and NO MILK! That is when I came to the conclusion that 1) I don't know how to milk a cow 2) I don't want to get kicked by a cow and 3) there was nothing "effortless" about the process. It's hard work, pure and simple.

The Neapolitan Proverbs

The Neapolitan proverbs that you will find throughout this book represent popular wisdom linked to a city with an ancient history and a cultural tradition unique in this world. These antique proverbs are rich with significant and invaluable lessons of life. They are born from life experiences and contain many indispensable teachings that are still followed today by current generations in modern day Neapolitan culture. These proverbs constitute, in some way, the history of Naples and Campania. They are centuries old and contain small pearls of wisdom representing the starting point of the education of those born in these towns.

The recipes I share with you are some of my personal favorites that have been passed down from one family member to another and originated from the imagination and creativity of the Campania and Neapolitan culinary culture. The name of each recipe has been written in English, followed by the Italian and Neapolitan versions. There are several typical holiday dishes but like many other Italians, we enjoy these specialties during other times of the year. Every recipe has a story with each region of Campania having its own version. These are our family traditional recipes, with a unique twist to bring our gluten-free specialties into the realm of deliciousness for everyone to enjoy!

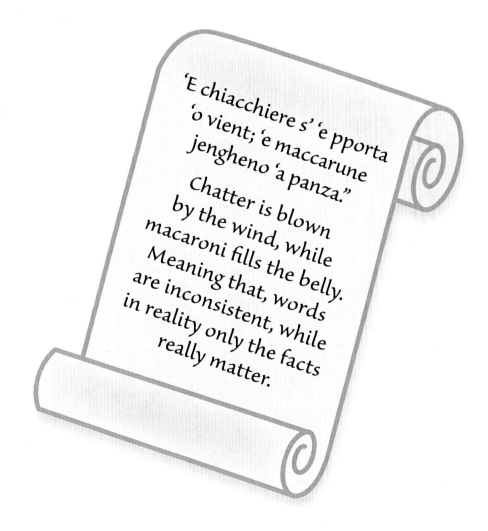

'E chiacchiere s' 'e pporta 'o vient; 'e maccarune jengheno 'a panza."

Chatter is blown by the wind, while macaroni fills the belly. Meaning that, words are inconsistent, while in reality only the facts really matter.

Rustic Neapolitan Appetizers

"Antipasti Rustici Napoletani"

The word "*Antipasti*" literally means "before the meal." Neapolitan rustic antipasti bring so much joy into your home in so many ways. In the Neapolitan traditions there is a long history of gastronomic preparations that combine classic sweet bases with savory ingredients, creating an original and exceptional encounter of flavors. It is a unique and true culinary art to combine sweet and savory in a perfect way. Some rustic recipes are simple while others need time and patience, but all are well worth it. These recipes can be enjoyed not only as appetizers, but also for lunch or dinner.

Fried Mini Pizzas (Pizzelle Fritte) 4

Potato Croquettes (Crocche' di Patate) 6

Twice Baked Bread with Beans (Friselle con Fagioli) 8

Fried Mini Pizzas
Pizzelle Fritte ('E pezzelle)

Yields: 6 to 8 (depending on size)
Prep Time: 10 minutes, plus 4 hours total resting time
Cook Time: 20 minutes

Some of the best things emerge in times of difficulty and fried mini pizza is one of them. After the Second World War, the Neapolitan people had little to eat. Everything was in short supply or impossible to find so the Neapolitan creativity came into play and the "princess" pizza, also known as a mini pizza, was created. It was easy to make and economical. These delightful and especially appetizing mini fried pizzas were born in the poorest neighborhoods of Naples and sold to those passing by, eventually becoming a sensational Neapolitan street food. If ever in the city streets of Naples, these are an absolute must! My sister Lucia makes the most amazing homemade version that always delights and amazes her guests. Together we began our quest to recreate gluten-free versions of these delicacies. After many attempts, we were finally able to create the perfect dough to make these little jewels. *Pizzelle Fritte* are loved by everyone so prepare many because they won't last!

Ingredients:

- 4 cups gluten-free all-purpose baking flour, plus more for dusting
- 4 tablespoons of psyllium husk
- 1 ½ teaspoons sea salt
- 1 tablespoon sugar
- 1 ½ teaspoons dry yeast
- 2 ½ cups warm water
- 2 tablespoons apple cider vinegar
- 2 ½ teaspoons extra virgin olive oil, plus more for oiling bowl
- 2 ½ pounds tomatoes-on-the-vine (about 8 to 12), cut in half
- Sea salt to taste
- 3 tablespoons extra virgin olive oil
- 2 cups cold-pressed canola or vegetable oil
- ½ cup freshly grated Parmigiano Reggiano or pecorino Romano cheese
- 6 to 8 fresh basil leaves, chopped, plus more for garnish

Directions:

For Pizza Dough:

1. In a large bowl mix together flour, psyllium husk, salt, sugar, and yeast.
2. In a separate bowl whisk together water, vinegar and olive oil. Slowly add liquid to flour and mix with your hands or a wooden spoon until the dough becomes homogeneous. Transfer dough to a lightly floured surface and knead for 5 minutes to form a round and smooth dough. Place dough in an oiled mixing bowl, cover with a clean kitchen towel and let rest in a warm part of the kitchen for two hours. When ready, roll dough on a lightly floured surface and divide into 6 to 8 even pieces, then roll each piece into a 6 to 7 inch disk and let rest for 2 more hours.

For Tomato Sauce:

3. Heat oil in a 3 quart pot. Add tomatoes, salt and simmer, covered, until wilted, about 5 to 10 minutes, stirring occasionally.
4. Place food mill over a second 3 quart pot and carefully transfer cooked tomatoes to the food mill. Once all the tomatoes have been processed, remove the food mill from the pot, bring tomato sauce to a boil on high heat, then lower heat to a simmer, add olive oil and salt to taste, and cook partially covered with a lid for 30 minutes. Stir in chopped basil.

For the Pizzelle:

5. Heat oil to in a large high-sided sauté pan to 300°F.
6. Place a paper-towel lined baking sheet tray next to the pot. When oil is hot, add pizzelle a few at a time so as not to crowd the pan. Gently turn with a fork or tongs until all sides are a deep golden brown, about 2 to 3 minutes on each side then transfer to towel-lined tray to drain.
7. Top with tomato sauce, grated pecorino or parmigiano, and garnish with basil leaves. Serve hot.

Notes:

You can use San Marzano tomato sauce in a glass jar (28 oz).

The oil temperature must be around 300°F before frying the pizzelle. If you do not have a kitchen thermometer, use a piece of dough as a test: dip it in the oil, if it bubbles then you can proceed with frying.

Potato Croquettes
Crocche' di Patate Napoletane ('E panzarotte)

Yields: 12 pieces (about 2 ½ ounces each)
Prep Time: 30 minutes
Cook Time: 45 minutes, plus frying time

In Italy these delicious little gems are known as *"Crocche' di Patate,"* but in Naples they are known as *"panzarotti,"* perhaps because of their pot-bellied shape resembling a soft and round "belly." According to some historians, the panzarotti date back to the 18th century where it was sold in the alleys of the historic center of Naples by the *"panzerottari"* (those who made them) and served hot in the *"cuoppo fritto,"* (paper cone), which typically holds a mix of deep-fried delicacies. Today these are still a famous street food in Naples and also enjoyed as appetizers or as an excellent side dish with meat and fish. Panzarotti are typically made with potatoes, eggs, prosciutto, and cheese, golden and crispy on the outside, soft and delicate on the inside. A guaranteed crowd pleaser!

Ingredients:

- 2 pounds Russet potatoes, washed
- 2 ¼ teaspoons sea salt, divided
- 3 large eggs, divided
- ¼ cup grated Parmigiano Reggiano cheese
- ¼ cup parsley, finely chopped
- Pinch black pepper freshly ground
- 1 ½ cups of organic canola oil or vegetable oil
- 2 ounces mozzarella cheese, small diced (about ¼" cubes)
- 2 ounces Prosciutto (or salami), roughly chopped
- 1 ½ cups organic cold-pressed canola or vegetable oil, as needed
- ¾ cups gluten-free bread crumbs

"A schizzi, a schizzi se fà 'o pantano." Drop by drop, the puddle forms. Meaning that with consistency and perseverance, regardless of obstacles, results that were initially unthinkable are obtained.

Directions:

1. Combine potatoes and 2 teaspoons salt in a large pot with enough water to cover. Bring to a boil, then simmer partially covered with a lid for 30 to 45 minutes until potatoes are fork-tender*. Set aside to cool then peel and pass through a potato ricer.
2. In a large bowl, add potatoes, one egg, parmigiano, parsley, pinch of salt, and black pepper. Mix together until well combined.
3. In a separate bowl mix together mozzarella and prosciutto. Set aside.
4. Line a baking sheet with parchment paper. Scoop about two and a half ounces of potato mixture and shape into a ball, press the center gently with your fingers and add about a teaspoon of the mozzarella and prosciutto mixture. Fold potato mixture over filling and gently roll into an oval shape so that filling is completely covered. Place croquette on baking sheet. Repeat until potato and filling mixtures are used up.

5. In a small bowl, whisk remaining eggs. In a separate bowl, add bread crumbs. Dip each croquette in egg, then roll in bread crumbs to cover, and return to baking sheet. Cover with plastic and refrigerate for 3 to 4 hours or overnight.

6. When ready to cook**, heat about 1-inch of oil in a high-sided pot to 350°F. Place a paper-towel lined baking sheet tray next to pot. When oil is hot, add croquettes a few at a time, leaving at least two inches of space around each one so as not to crowd the pan. This prevents the croquettes from crumbling while frying. Gently turn with a fork or tongs until all sides are brown, about 2 to 3 minutes on each side then transfer to towel-lined tray to drain. Continue with remaining oil and croquettes until they are all cooked. Season with remaining salt to taste and serve hot or at room temperature.

Notes:

Be careful not to overcook potatoes or it will be more difficult to shape croquettes.

**To bake instead of frying, after breading croquettes, place them on a parchment-lined baking sheet, cover with plastic and refrigerate for 30 minutes, then drizzle croquettes with extra virgin olive oil, and bake at 395°F for 15 to 20 minutes until browned and heated through.*

Twice Baked Bread with Beans
Friselle con Fagioli (E freselle cu' e' fasul)

> Yields: 8 servings
> Prep Time: 20 minutes, plus 2 hours 40 minutes
> of resting time plus bean soaking time
> Baking Time: 1 hour

"*La Frisella*" is one of the most well-known and appreciated culinary specialties from the Campania, a true gastronomic symbol of the South. It was once created from stale bread and considered an expression of poor, peasant Neapolitan cuisine where nothing was ever thrown away. Crumbs of bread, even if hardened, were saved in order to have food on the table. According to historians, street vendors called "*tarallari*" sold their "*friselle*" in the streets of Naples in the 1300's. The shape of friselle was created for specific transport and storage needs. In fact, friselle were inserted onto a string whose ends were knotted to form a necklace, making it easy to hang, dry, transport and store. They were considered a travel bread because it lasted for several days thus making it a common food during fishing trips. The fisherman would bathe the friselle in seawater or use them as a base for fish or mussel soup.

Friselle have a long shelf-life and are fantastically versatile. They are perfect for impromptu bruschetta or can be added to your favorite soup, for example. Friselle are usually seasoned with tomatoes, oregano, basil, garlic, and olive oil, but you can indulge yourself with the most varied ingredients depending on what you are in the mood for. When we prepared them we were in the mood for cooked beans, olive oil, and garlic! Neapolitan style is to quickly wet it under running water, or in this case, dipped quickly in the cooked bean juice and then seasoned at will. Here is our recipe for homemade, simple, light, and delicious gluten-free friselle with beans. When homemade their shape is similar to that of bagels.

Ingredients:

- 1 pound dry cannellini beans, soaked overnight in enough water to cover, refrigerated
- 2 teaspoons sea salt, divided, plus more to season before serving
- 1 ½ teaspoons fresh yeast
- 1 ¼ cups warm water
- 4 tablespoons extra virgin olive oil, divided, plus more for drizzling
- 3 ¼ cups gluten-free all-purpose baking flour, plus more for dusting
- 2 garlic cloves, chopped

Directions:

For Beans:

1. Discard any beans that have floated to the surface of the soaking water. Then drain and rinse with cold water.
2. Transfer beans to a two-quart Dutch oven and cover with fresh water. There should be about 2 inches of water above the beans. Bring to a boil, then lower heat and simmer, covered for 1½ to 2 hours, stirring occasionally, until beans are tender but still keep their shape. Stir in one teaspoon of salt when beans are finished cooking.

For Friselle:

3. Prepare a baking sheet with parchment paper and set aside.
4. In a medium-size bowl add yeast to warm water and mix with a spatula until yeast is dissolved. Stir in two tablespoons of extra virgin olive oil. Set aside for 10 minutes.
5. Place flour and one teaspoon of salt in large bowl. Slowly add yeast mixture. Gently stir using a rubber spatula until you have a homogeneous mixture. Cover with plastic wrap and let rise in a warm part of the kitchen for 2 hours or until dough has doubled in size.
6. When dough is ready, transfer to a floured work surface. Lightly flour your hands and gently roll dough into a log about nine inches long and four inches wide. Cut into ten equal pieces with a bench scraper. Roll each piece into an eight inch strip, then join the ends and press lightly so that they stick together to form a thick circle*.
7. Arrange friselle on the prepared baking sheet, leaving about two inches between each one. Cover with a clean kitchen towel and let rise in a warm part of the kitchen for 40 minutes.
8. Preheat the oven to 425°F.
9. Lightly brush the top of each friselle with remaining extra virgin olive oil and bake for 20 minutes. Set aside to cool.
10. While friselle cool, lower the oven temperature to 335°F.
11. Cut each friselle in half horizontally with a serrated knife. Place them back on the baking sheet, cut-side up, and bake for 40 minutes until deeply golden on both sides. Turn sheet pan 180° in the oven halfway through the cooking so that all sides bake evenly. Allow to cool completely before serving. If not using right away completely cooled friselle can be stored at room temperature in clear food bags for up to four weeks.

To Serve:

12. Soak friselle halves in bean cooking liquid and place open-faced on individual plates or serving platter. Top each frizzle half with about ½ cup of beans, followed by chopped garlic, and a pinch each of salt and black pepper. Drizzle with extra virgin olive oil and serve.

Notes:

To prepare friselle with a more traditional topping: per serving, mix together one plum tomato, chopped, along with a pinch of dried oregano, 1 fresh basil leaf, chopped, 2 tablespoons extra virgin olive oil, and salt and pepper to taste. Quickly dip each friselle in a bowl filled with cold water and place on a serving platter open-faced. Drizzle friselle with olive oil, top with tomato mixture, and garnish with chopped garlic and fresh basil leaves.

*Instead of rings, form friselle into rolls and bake at 425°F for 30 to 40 minutes, or until golden brown.

Salads

"Insalate"

According to historians, salads originated in Italy during the 14th century and were seasoned simply with oil, vinegar, and salt. Over the centuries, imagination has turned salads into colorful, healthy, and refreshing meals made up of a medley of ingredients. Our family likes to serve a refreshing simple salad during our meals, much like the original version. Our salad is prepared the same traditional way or we substitute vinegar with lemon. A good salad goes well with almost any dish. We tend to eat our salads with or after the second dish (secondo piatto) to help improve digestion and to cleanse our palate. There are also special salads that are specifically prepared for holiday meals.

Cod Salad (L'insalata di Baccala') 12

Reinforcement Salad (L'insalata di Rinforzo) 14

Cod Salad
L'insalata di Baccala' ('A 'nzalata 'e baccala')

Yields: 4 servings
Prep Time: 15 minutes, plus 3 to 4 days soaking time
Cook Time: 20 minutes

Cod salad is a traditional, Neapolitan dish that is typically enjoyed on Christmas Eve. It is one of my favorite dishes that I can eat daily and that is why we make this spectacular dish throughout the year. At Christmas time we add additional ingredients such as cauliflower and pickled *"papacelle"* (small, squat Italian peppers - refer to page 61). *"L'insalata di Baccala"* is a cod salad that is simple to make. The Neapolitan tradition is to eat cold cod with olives, parsley, lemon, garlic, and extra virgin olive oil, all of which enhance the flavor of this delicious and healthy dish. The cod is preserved with heavy salt and must be soaked for a few days and changing the water 3 times a day eliminates the excess salt. As with many traditional recipes, its presence on Neapolitan tables at Christmas time is indispensable!

Ingredients:

- 2 pounds salt cod, cut into 3-inch pieces
- 1 garlic clove, chopped
- 1 cup green or black olives, or a combination
- 3 tablespoons extra virgin olive oil
- Juice of one small lemon
- 2 tablespoons fresh parsley, chopped

"'A bbona campana se sente 'a luntano." The good bell can be heard from afar. Meaning that when something is done well, you notice it immediately.

Directions:

1. Soak cod for 3 to 4 days, refrigerated, changing water 2 to 3 times a day. In a large pot bring 6 quarts of water to boil, add cod ensuring that the cod is completely covered. Bring back to a boil, then lower heat and simmer covered for 15 to 20 minutes. Strain and cool. After it cools, remove skin and bones, if there are any, and break into bite size pieces with a fork.
2. In a mixing bowl, add cod, garlic, olives, olive oil, and lemon juice. Gently mix together until well combined. Cover with plastic and store in the refrigerator one hour before serving.
3. Place in serving platter and garnish with parsley.

Notes:

Soaked cod can be stored in the freezer for up to six weeks.

Store leftover cod salad in an airtight container refrigerated for two to three days.

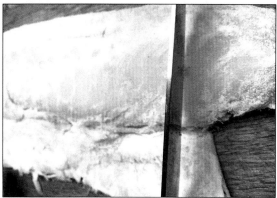

Reinforcement Salad
L'insalata di Rinforzo ('A 'nzalata 'e rinforzo)

Yields: 4 servings
Prep Time: 20 minutes, plus 1 hour resting time
Cook time: 15 minutes

This is a traditional Neapolitan culinary dish, originating in the 17th century. The masters of the kitchen prepared it in a simpler way than how we are used to eating it today. The traditional recipe has gone through so many changes that it has become difficult to establish the exact ingredients. It is a family favorite that is served primarily from Christmas Eve through New Years Day. Since the traditional Christmas Eve dinner is not a light one, the reinforcement salad was added to provide *"rinforzo"* (reinforcement) in order to balance the meal. As my family always states, (it is a salad that will help you digest and make room for more). In other words, it wets your appetite! There are various interpretations based on the origin of this unique name. In this case, reinforcement means the presence of fairly substantial ingredients that accompany meals based on seafood dishes. Traditionally, it is made with cauliflower, *"papacelle"* (refer to page 61), olives, capers, and anchovies. We added other vegetables to the mix, such as carrots and celery, and since papacelle are sometimes difficult to find in the United States, we substituted with beautiful red and orange peppers.

Ingredients:

- 1 medium cauliflower, cut into florets
- 4 celery stalks, cut into 1½ inch-thick pieces
- 2 medium-sized carrots, peeled and cut into ½ inch-thick rounds
- 2 red and orange peppers, cored, deseeded, and cut into ½-inch thick squares
- 3 cups white wine vinegar
- 3 cups filtered water
- 2 teaspoons sea salt

To prepare the salad:

1. Cooked vegetables
2. 2 garlic cloves, thinly sliced
3. 1/3 cup extra virgin olive oil
4. 1/4 teaspoon oregano
5. 1 tablespoon capers
6. 1/2 cup whole black olives (or/and green olives), rinsed
7. 6 anchovy fillets
8. Sea salt to taste
9. Black pepper, freshly ground, to taste

Directions:

To make quick-pickled vegetables:

1. In a medium saucepan, combine vinegar and water and bring to a simmer over low heat, then add salt. Place a large baking sheet lined with a clean kitchen-towel next to the pan.
2. Add cauliflower, return to a simmer and cook for 2 minutes. Drain with a spider strainer and transfer to the prepared baking sheet. Add celery and cook for 3 minutes, drain and transfer to baking sheet. Add carrots, cook for 3 minutes, drain and transfer to baking sheet. Lastly, add peppers, cook for 3 minutes, drain and transfer to baking sheet. Set aside to cool.

To prepare the salad:

3. Place vegetables in a large bowl and gently mix together with garlic, olive oil, oregano, capers, olives, anchovies, sea salt and black pepper. Cover with plastic and store in the refrigerator for an hour or overnight to allow flavors to marry.
4. Serve cold topped with additional anchovies and a sprinkle of extra virgin olive oil.

Notes:

Store salad in an airtight container refrigerated for two to three days.

Soups of the Campania Region

"Zuppe della Campania"

"*Le Zuppe*"(soups) are true masterpieces of taste and wisdom, created with few ingredients and little technique culminating in extraordinary results. They are very fragrant and healthy dishes that are highly sought after.

Soups are the saviors of the soul - emotionally, physically and spiritually, and can warm the body and give it the energy it needs. Each region of Campania has its own methods of preparation and flavoring. With a little imagination, sensational recipes are created. There is a difference, however, between "*zuppa*" and "*minestra*". The main distinction between the two lies in the presence or absence of rice or pasta. Zuppa is primarily a broth without rice or pasta and is often served with homemade toasted bread. In fact, the name zuppa derives from the Gothic "*suppa*" meaning a slice of soaked bread. Pieces of stale bread are usually placed on the bottom of the bowls before pouring the soup. Minestra, on the other hand, usually includes vegetables and legumes with the addition of rice or pasta.

Today things have changed quite a bit and preparing zuppa or minestra is all about imagination linked to the culinary traditions of a region, local crops, seasons, and personal tastes.

Lentil Soup (Zuppa di Lenticchie) *18*

Pizza, Beans, and Vegetable Soup (Pizza, Fasul, e Minestra)...............................*20*

The Wedding Soup (Minestra Maritata) *22*

Lentil Soup
Zuppa di Lenticchie ('A zupp 'e' lenticchie)

> Yields: 4 to 6 servings
> Prep Time: 20 minutes
> Cook Time: 50 minutes

A simple, healthy and delicious Mediterranean delicacy that is full of nutrients. According to historians, lentils were cultivated as early as 525 BC in the land of ancient Egypt and are the oldest legume. They were the first in history to be grown and the first to be cooked eventually spreading throughout the Mediterranean, becoming a staple food of the Greeks and Romans. Thanks to affordability and easy availability, they were called "the poor man's steak" because lentils were considered a nutritious and substantial food capable of feeding and supporting those who could not afford to consume meat and expensive foods.

"Zuppa di Lenticchie" is a typical first-course meal in Southern Italy. It is a tasty dish that is capable of warming you during cold winter days, as well as energizing you due to its nutritious content. Lentils have always been a family favorite legume used in various recipes and in many different ways. They are easier to digest, are free of fats and cholesterol and are rich in many vitamins and minerals. Lentil soup is a comfort food that can be served dry or soupy and the legume cooking water can be used to dip delicious toasted rustic bread. Traditionally, Neapolitans typically add small, short, mixed pasta or even broken spaghetti to lentil soup. Either way, it's irresistible and a perfect dish to be enjoyed at any time!

Legend has it that eating lentils on New Year's Eve ensures a year of good fortune. A spoonful of lentils is eaten before the toast at the last stroke of midnight. The more you eat, the more good fortune you will have. I've done this myself many times and I believe it works!

Ingredients:

- 16 ounce dry lentils, rinsed
- 4 tablespoons extra virgin olive oil
- 1 celery stalk, small diced (about 2 ounces)
- ½ large carrot, small diced (about 3 ounces)
- 2 large plum tomatoes, chopped
- 3 garlic cloves, whole
- 1/8 cup fresh parsley leaves, whole
- 2 liters of water (about 9 cups)
- Sea salt to taste
- Ground black pepper to taste

Directions:

1. Rinse lentils under running water and set aside.
2. Heat oil in a six-quart Dutch oven, add celery and carrots and sauté for 2 minutes. Add lentils, tomatoes, garlic, parsley and water and stir. Bring to a boil, then reduce heat and simmer covered for 40 minutes or until lentils are tender. Add salt and pepper to taste.

Notes:

If pressed for time use organic canned lentils instead, rinsed well. Taste of the lentils will be different.

If you would like to add pasta to this dish, we suggest using gluten-free "Ditalini" pasta (about 12 ounces) for this recipe.

Store lentil soup in an airtight container and refrigerated for about 3 days. Otherwise, store in the freezer and use within 2 months.

Corn Pizza, Beans, and Vegetable Soup
Pizza, Fasul, e Minestra ('A minestr 'ca piz e fasul)

> Yields: 8 servings
> Prep Time: 40 minutes, plus bean soaking time
> Cook Time: 35 to 45 minutes, plus 1½ to 2 hours
> bean cooking time

Traditionally *"Pizza, Fasul, e Minestra"* is a Neapolitan soup known as *"pignato magro."* A simple, delicious, nutritious, warm and welcoming dish that always brings back memories of my nonna's kitchen. It is a recipe that is particularly appreciated during the winter months and is usually served in a classic terracotta dish, which makes this creation even more rustic and genuine. In Campania it is considered a classic peasant dish because the rustic flavors bring to the table all the authenticity of the past. Pizza, Fasul, e Minestra lacked meat so it was a dish of the most destitute. Destitute or not, it will amaze you with all its goodness. It's also nutritious and healthy, where the sweetness of cannellini beans meets the bitter taste of escarole, and is served with delicious and crunchy baked corn pizza. Flawless!

Ingredients:

For beans:

- 1 pound cannellini beans, soaked overnight in enough water to cover, refrigerated*
- Fresh water for cooking
- 1 bay leaf
- 1 teaspoon sea salt

For corn pizza:

- 8 cups water
- 1 ½ teaspoon sea salt
- 2 cups yellow cornmeal, plus 1 ½ tablespoons to top off pizza before baking

For minestra:

- 4 heads escarole, (about 3 to 4 pounds), trimmed
- 3 pounds chicory, trimmed
- 1 pound dandelion greens, trimmed (optional)
- 1/3 cup extra virgin olive oil, plus more for greasing
- 3 to 4 garlic cloves, peeled and whole
- Pinch red crushed pepper
- 4 cups cooked cannellini beans, reserving the liquid
- 1 teaspoon sea salt, plus more to taste
- Freshly grated Parmigiano Reggiano or pecorino Romano, for garnish

Directions:

For beans:

1. Discard any beans that have floated to the surface of the soaking water. Then drain and rinse with cold water.
2. Transfer beans to a Dutch oven. Cover with water by 1 to 2 inches above level of beans, add bay leaf and bring to a boil. Turn down heat, and simmer covered for 1½ to 2 hours, until tender, stirring occasionally. When beans are cooked add salt. Set aside.

For Pizza:

3. Preheat oven to 375°F. Grease a large baking tray with a bit of olive oil, cover with parchment paper, and grease again.
4. In a gallon pot, bring water and salt to a boil. Reduce heat to medium and slowly add cornmeal in a steady stream, whisking frequently until you have a thick consistency and is not excessively soft like polenta, about 10 to 15 minutes.
5. Transfer cooked cornmeal to prepared baking sheet, sprinkle with a little extra virgin olive oil and spread evenly to a thickness of about ½ inch all over using a rubber spatula. Use wet hands to evenly flatten the pizza then add reserved 1½ tablespoons of cornmeal to the top and bake for 1 to 1½ hours, turning the tray halfway through, until it begins to brown and crisp on edges.

For minestra:

6. Bring a large pot of water to boil with a pinch of salt. Blanch escarole and chicory (and dandelion leaves, if using) for 3 to 4 minutes. Cut in halves and set aside.
7. In a Dutch oven or deep-sided frying pan, add olive oil, garlic, and red pepper and sauté until garlic turns a golden brown. Add escarole, chicory, beans with cooking liquid and salt. Bring to a boil then lower to a simmer and cook covered for 45 minutes to an hour, or until greens are tender. If too dry, add a little boiling water.
8. Cut corn pizza into sixteen 2-inch by 2-inch squares and place two squares in each of eight soup bowls. Top with the *fasul e minestra* mixture. Garnish with pecorino Romano or Parmigiano Reggiano cheese.

Notes:

Store leftovers in an airtight container refrigerated for two to three days. Store leftover pizza separately in plastic wrap for two days; reheat in the oven before adding to the dish.

If you have leftover beans, freeze in a plastic container, leaving a few inches of space at the top to allow for expansion, for two to three weeks. Do not store beans in a glass container since beans tend to expand when frozen and they can shatter the glass.

*You can skip this step and use organic canned beans.

Wedding Soup
Minestra Maritata ('A menesta'mmaretata)

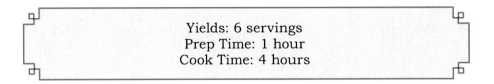

Yields: 6 servings
Prep Time: 1 hour
Cook Time: 4 hours

According to historians, "*Minestra Maritata*" is a Neapolitan dish with many ancient origins and is believed to be the oldest Neapolitan cuisine. It is a traditional soup known as "*il matrimonio tra carne e verdura*" (marriage between meat and vegetables); a marriage that has been together for many centuries. Beginning in the 16th century, the term "*maritata*" derived from the union of different ingredients which "marry" perfectly, as in this soup, Minestra Maritata. This incredibly delicious dish is generally prepared during festive lunches. Each recipe varies and ingredients have been modified over the years but it is based on mixed vegetables such as escarole, chicory, cabbage, borage and such meats as pork, sausages and chicken. Like any regional recipe, even the "Wedding Soup" boasts numerous variations, which differs from one home to another. It is a dish that takes a lot of patience and time but well worth it!

My mamma shared with me that when she was young there was no refrigeration and meat was expensive and considered a delicacy. In order to enjoy these specialties themselves, they would go to the butcher at closing time because the butcher would sell leftover scraps of meat at especially low prices. With these scraps, they created this wonderful soup full of flavor and nutrients. Since they were only able to purchase small amounts of these meats, they used the scraps, along with whatever vegetables they had and created this amazing dish.

Ingredients:

- 7 quarts of water

- Half a chicken (1½-2 pounds)
- 1 ½ pounds of beef (chuck, roast, or stewing beef)
- 1 pound sweet sausages
- 2 medium-sized carrots, peeled
- 3 celery stalks
- 1 onion, peeled
- 10 sprigs of parsley
- 4 garlic cloves
- 3 bay leaves
- 1 plum tomato, chopped

- 1 pound of chicory greens
- 1 pound escarole
- ½ pound green cabbage, cored, cut in thick wedges
- 1 pound Swiss chard, trimmed
- 1 pound broccoli rabe, trimmed
- 1 pound dandelion greens, trimmed
- ½ pound of kale (or borage)
- ¼ pound freshly grated Parmigiano Reggiano or Pecorino Romano cheese

Directions:

1. In a large pot, add water, chicken, beef, sausages, and whole carrots, celery, onion, parsley, garlic cloves, bay leaves, and chopped tomato. Bring to a boil on high heat, then lower heat and simmer for 3½ to 4 hours.

2. While soup cooks, trim and discard ends and any brown leaves from greens (chicory, escarole, cabbage, chard, broccoli rabe, dandelion, and kale or borage). Do not mix greens together. Bring a large pot of water to a boil and cook each type of greens separately for 3 to 5 minutes each, depending on their toughness. Set cooked greens aside on a baking sheet. Once cooled, cut each green in half.

3. When soup has finished cooking, remove chicken, meat, and sausage and cut into bite-size pieces (about ¾ to 1").

4. Strain broth through a large sieve into a second large pot. Discard parsley, bay leaves, and tomatoes. Place carrots, onions, and celery on the side (these can be sliced and served alongside soup with some extra virgin olive oil, salt and pepper to taste).

5. Add meats and greens to soup and bring to a boil. Turn down heat and simmer for another 40 minutes.

6. To serve, ladle soup into bowls, top each with cheese and enjoy with toasted rustic Italian bread.

Notes:

Store cooled soup in an airtight container refrigerated for two to three days. Or freeze for two to three weeks in a plastic container or freezer bag, leaving a few inches of space at the top to allow for expansion. Do not store and freeze in a glass container as the glass may shatter.

Pasta, Pizza, and Sauces

"La Pasta, Pizza, e Sughi"

$\mathcal{P}$asta and pizza is serious business in Italy. I remember many years ago, if not making their own homemade pasta, my grandparents would purchase fresh pasta by the kilo wrapped up in brown paper. The all-Italian enthusiasm for pasta was born in Naples in the 17th century. It became the dish of choice for the people who began to eat it when the price of flour fell and that of meat skyrocketed. The origin of pizza was somewhere between the 16th and 17th centuries in Naples. The marriage of pizza and tomatoes was born in the 18th century, when the Neapolitan pizza makers began using tomatoes and it quickly conquered the palate of all people including royalty. The Margherita pizza was dedicated and named after Queen Margherita of Savoy and eventually became the most famous and most celebrated pizza in the world. This pizza is a simple preparation that represents the colors of the Italian flag: basil for green, mozzarella for white, and tomatoes for red. As they say, the rest is history....

There are several Campania sauces that our family has thoroughly enjoyed for many years, some of which I have included in this book. Traditionally, most of the sauce preparations included tomatoes, which according to historians, entered the culinary world around the 18th century. To this day, the sauces of Campania still include an abundant amount of tomatoes, especially on Sundays when we have our traditional family gatherings!

Escarole Pie (Pizza di Scarola) 26

Genovese Sauce (Sugo alla Genovese) 28

Macaroni Frittata (Frittata di Maccheroni) 30

Meat Based Tomato Sauce (Ragù Napoletano) 32

Pasta, Potatoes, and Provola (Pasta, Patate, e Provola) 34

Tagliatelle Pasta and Beans (Tagliatelle e Fagioli) 36

Escarole Pie
Pizza di Scarola Napoletana ('A pizz e' scarol)

Yields: 6 to 8 slices
Prep Time: 30 minutes, plus 2 hours resting time
Cook Time: 1 hour 30 minutes

The Neapolitan *"Pizza di Scarola"* is a rustic dish of tradition and culinary culture symbolic at Christmas time in the Campania region, but is quite suitable for any occasion. There are variations of this sweet and savory delight, and it is this particularity that makes it a unique and special dish. Historically, it was known as *"Pizza con la jeta"* or chard, which we still use at times. In our Neapolitan household, especially during the festive period, it is a tradition to enrich the tables with this delicacy. According to my family, it is a typical dish that was born in the period of poverty. Historians believe that it originated around the 1600's and still is one of the most requested dishes on Christmas Eve in order to satisfy hunger pangs while waiting for the holiday seafood extravaganza. We eat a slice of pizza with escarole to keep us satisfied but there is only one slight problem - one slice always leads to another!

Ingredients:

For pizza

- 4 cups gluten-free all-purpose baking flour, plus more for dusting
- 4 tablespoons of psyllium husk
- 1 ½ teaspoons sea salt
- 1 tablespoon sugar
- 1 ½ teaspoons dry yeast
- 2 ½ cups warm water
- 2 tablespoons apple cider vinegar
- 2 ½ teaspoons extra virgin olive oil, plus more for oiling bowls
- 1 bottle extra virgin olive oil spray

For escarole

- 4 pounds escarole, washed three times and spun dry
- 2 gallons cold water
- 1/3 cup extra virgin olive oil
- 3 garlic cloves, sliced*
- Pinch of crushed red pepper
- ½ cup golden raisins
- ¼ cup pine nuts
- ½ cup chopped Gaeta black olives
- Sea salt to taste
- 1 teaspoon extra virgin olive oil

Directions:

For dough

1. In a large bowl mix together flour, psyllium husk, salt, sugar, and yeast.
2. In a separate bowl whisk together water, vinegar, and olive oil. Slowly add liquid to flour and mix with hands until the dough becomes homogeneous. Transfer dough to a lightly floured surface and knead for 5 minutes to form a round and smooth dough. Divide dough in half and place each piece in separate lightly oiled bowls, cover each bowl with a kitchen towel and let rest in a warm part of the kitchen for two hours. When ready, roll each half on a lightly floured surface into a 10 to 12 inch disc.

For escarole

3. While dough rests bring water to a boil in a large pot. Add escarole and cook at a rolling boil for 6 to 7 minutes, drain and set aside.

4. Heat oil in a large high-sided sauté pan, add garlic and red pepper, and sauté until garlic turns a golden brown. Add escarole and cook for 5 minutes more. Add raisins, pine nuts, black olives and salt to taste and sauté for 15 minutes, stirring occasionally. Remove from pan and set aside.

To bake

5. Preheat oven to 400°F.

6. Grease the bottom of a 9-inch round or springform pan with olive oil spray. Place one disk of dough in the pan and gently massage dough to the pan's edges until the bottom is completely covered. Top with escarole and cover with the second dough round. Pull top dough gently to completely cover greens. Flatten with wet fingers and press down lightly around edges to seal. Brush top with extra virgin olive oil. Cover with a clean kitchen towel and rest in a warm part of the kitchen for 30 minutes.

7. When ready, bake for 1 hour. Cool for 15 minutes before serving. Pizza di Scarola is delicious hot, warm, or at room temperature.

Notes:

To serve as an appetizer or snack, prepare recipe in a square pan.

*If you prefer to discard garlic after escarole is finished cooking leave cloves whole.

Genovese Sauce
Sugo alla Genovese ('A sarza 'a genoese)

Yields: 6 servings
Prep Time: 30 minutes
Cooking Time: 2 hours 20 minutes

Despite the name, Genovese pasta is a Neapolitan tradition and a typical first course and equally important as that of the ragù. The origin of the name has various theories. Some believe that it stemmed from the Genovese cooks who gathered in the streets of Naples in the 16th century cooking meat-based sauces with which to season the pasta. Nourishment for the soul! Every Neapolitan family has its own secret recipe for this sauce and even if there are different versions, the ingredients that remain the same are onion, meat and pasta. Today, the recipe most likely dates back to the second half of the 19th century and is considered the poor version of the classic ragù. Genovese sauce can be considered a white ragù with the addition of many onions, which are cooked over low heat for a long time until they soften and create an exquisite creamy puree with a sweet but decisive flavor. It is one of my absolute favorites and although traditionally prepared with "*mezzanilli*" pasta or "*ziti spezzati*," meaning pasta broken by hand, it will taste great with any pasta of your choice. In our recipe we used gluten-free "*casarecce*" pasta!

Traditionally, our family makes the sauce by thinly slicing onions and cooking them for a long period of time with other ingredients. Below is the recipe that my family has used for as long as I can remember. My mamma also created a different version so that, in her own words, "*ci sono meno lacrime*," which means there are less tears. The only difference in the recipes is how the onions are cut and cooked. The rest remains the same. Either way, this dish is absolutely superb!

Our Traditional Recipe:

Ingredients:

- ⅓ cup extra virgin olive oil
- 1½ pounds onions, thinly sliced
- 10 cherry tomatoes, cut in half
- 2 stalks celery, minced (about 3/4 cup)
- 2 medium -sized carrots, minced (about 1 cup)
- 1 pound of veal (can sub with lean beef), cut into 3 evenly sized pieces
- ½ teaspoon sea salt, divided
- ½ cup extra virgin olive oil
- Sea salt to taste
- Black pepper, freshly ground, to taste
- 1½ pounds gluten-free pasta (ziti, rigatoni, or casarecce)
- ¼ cup freshly grated Parmigiano Reggiano or pecorino Romano, to taste

Directions:

1. Heat oil in a large high-sided sauté pan, add onions and cook on medium-low heat until onions are soft and translucent,about 1 hour. Then, remove from heat and puree for 1 minute using an immersion blender. Return to medium-low heat and add tomatoes, celery, carrots, veal, and ¼ teaspoon of salt. Cover and cook for 1 hour 30 minutes, stirring occasionally. Remove cover and cook for another 30 minutes to get a creamy consistency.
2. Bring a large pot of water to a boil and add pasta, following cooking instructions for al dente. Drain and place back in the pot. Add 1 to 2 ladles of Genovese sauce and mix well.
3. Serve hot topped with additional Genovese sauce and freshly grated cheese.

Mamma's Version: Use same ingredients as above.

Directions for Onions:

1. Peel and cut onions in quarters.
2. Bring 2 cups of water to a boil in a large pot and add the onions. Stir and cook onions uncovered for 10 minutes, until they are soft.
3. Place onions in a food processor or blender and puree into a cream, about 30 seconds. Do not over blend. The onions should be thick and creamy.
4. In a large Dutch oven add olive oil, pureed onions, tomatoes, celery, carrots, veal, and cook covered for 1 hour 30 minutes, then remove cover and cook for another 30 minutes.

Notes:

You can store leftover Genovese sauce in an airtight container and in the refrigerator for 2 days. Or freeze in an airtight container for 1 month.

Genovese sauce can be used to prepare "Lasagna alla Genovese."

To make it vegetarian, simply remove the meat.

Macaroni Frittata
Frittata di Maccheroni (A' frittat 'e maccarun)

> Yields: 6 servings
> Prep Time: 10 minutes
> Cooking Time: 30 minutes

One of my favorite dishes for leftover past of any kind! The stereotype of the Neapolitan "*mangiamaccheroni*" (macaroni eaters) is at least three centuries old. It is a nickname given to the Neapolitan people in the 1800's for their love of pasta. This recipe is neither a first or second dish. It is simply a unique and tasty frittata made typically on Sundays from leftover pasta, when lunch was prepared in excess amounts because Italians always seem to have surprise guests! This is a recipe so dear to mothers and grandmothers from Campania that can be made white or red, in other words with or without sauce or tomatoes. Macaroni frittata is usually prepared with eggs, cheese, especially scamorza or parmigiano, pancetta, prosciutto (bacon) or whatever you have in the fridge. You can also make this dish with freshly cooked pasta such as penne, rigatoni, spaghetti, linguini, or bucatini. The ingredients can be imaginatively replaced according to your taste buds. A substantial and truly delicious dish that we have enjoyed at the beach and family picnics. In my opinion, it's perfect at any time and even better if eaten cold!

In the month of May, my mamma's garden tends to grow an abundant amount of "*rugola*", or as we know it, arugula. My friends in the UK call it rocket. Rugola is a vegetable with many names, many benefits and many uses. I decided to make rugola pesto, which is one of my favorite ways to use rugola because it is so versatile. I originally made it to serve on crostini as an appetizer for guests but quite a bit remained so we prepared pasta with rugola pesto for a Sunday lunch instead of the traditional ragù. We used gluten-free linguini for this dish and with the additional leftover pasta decided to make "*La Frittata di Maccheroni*" with it. We had additional rugola pesto leftover as well and since this is one of my favorite dishes, we cooked more linguini, added it to the remaining pasta and rugola pesto and voilà, a perfect Frittata di Maccheroni! As mentioned, you can add your heart's desire to this special dish. Below is the recipe using the leftover rugola pesto and linguini. Enjoy!

Ingredients:

- 1 pound gluten-free linguini (leftover or cooked pasta)
- 1 cup arugula pesto, more if needed
- 6 large eggs
- 1 cup freshly grated pecorino Romano or Parmigiano Reggiano, grated
- Sea salt to taste
- Black pepper, freshly ground, to taste
- ¼ cup extra virgin olive oil

Directions:

1. Bring a large pot of water to boil, add a pinch of salt and pasta. Cook pasta following the time indicated for al dente. When cooked, strain and set aside to cool. (Begin at this point if using leftover past)
2. In a large bowl mix together pasta and arugula pesto.
3. In a separate bowl mix together eggs, cheese, and salt and pepper to taste. Add pasta to the mixture and mix well.
4. Heat oil in a large high-sided nonstick sauté pan. Add pasta mixture and flatten top with a rubber spatula. Cook on medium heat until the bottom is golden brown, about 15 minutes. If there are any pools of liquid, use a fork to prod it so that the liquid goes to the bottom. Run a spatula around the sides of the frittata to loosen it. Place a flat lid or plate on top and quickly invert the frittata onto the lid or plate. Slide the frittata back into the pan, uncooked side down.* Cook on medium heat until bottom is golden brown. Remove from heat and let the frittata stand for 2 minutes. Using a rubber spatula, loosen the frittata from the skillet and slide the frittata onto a plate.
5. Cut frittata into wedges and serve. Enjoy hot or cold!

Notes:

Cover leftover frittata with plastic, or in an airtight container, refrigerated for up to 2 days. Freezing is not recommended.

*If you are uncomfortable flipping the frittata, heat oven to 375°F, cook one side on stop top, then place pan in the oven and cook until the top is golden brown, about 15 minutes.

How to make rugola pesto:

Ingredients:

- 2 cups rugola leaves, washed
- 1 cup extra virgin olive oil
- ½ cup pine nuts
- 1 tablespoon fresh lemon juice
- ½ cup pecorino Romano or Parmigiano Reggiano
- 1 garlic clove, chopped
- 1 teaspoon sea salt

Directions:

1. Wash the rugola well, dry it and place in a food processor. Add pine nuts, garlic, lemon juice, cheese, salt and pulse to blend. With the machine running, slowly pour in the olive oil through the food tube in a slow, steady stream and process until smooth, about 2 to 3 minutes, stopping to scrape down the sides of the bowl as needed. You may not need the entire amount of olive oil.
2. Taste and adjust seasoning.

Meat Based Tomato Sauce
Ragu Napoletano ('O rrau')

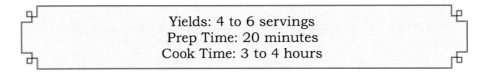

Yields: 4 to 6 servings
Prep Time: 20 minutes
Cook Time: 3 to 4 hours

The king of the Campania cuisine and a characteristic Sunday dish of Naples is the ragù. This is a dish that requires patience and passion, with an explosion of flavors that are tasty and completely unique. It is a sauce that makes you feel in harmony with the world! This type of sauce differs from the many Italian variations in the ingredients, preparation and care that it requires so there is no real recipe. For instance, there is variation in the choice of meat and tomatoes to be used, pureed or peeled. At times our family adds pig skin to the ragù. My grandparents would first boil the pig skin and then prepare it similar to the preparation of the braciole. If you desire, use an 8 ounce pig skin for this recipe. Our family also makes homemade tomato sauce and bottles it for the year. It's what I was raised with, never having to purchase a can or bottle of tomato sauce. Regardless of the version, a nice plate of *"macaroni"* with this phenomenally flavorful ragù and sprinkled with a generous handful of grated pecorino cheese is completely irresistible.

From this one dish, you can make a two course meal by adding the ragù to pasta as a first course and utilizing the meats as a second course. Complete the meal with a refreshing salad, which also acts as a side dish to cleanse your palate and help you digest.

Ingredients:

- 1½ pounds beef braciole
- 1½ pounds pork loin, pounded
- ½ cup fresh Parmigiano Reggiano or pecorino Romano, grated
- 4 garlic cloves, minced
- ⅓ cup fresh parsley, chopped
- Pinch Sea salt to taste, plus more to taste
- Pepper to taste
- ¼ cup extra virgin olive oil
- 1 medium onion, small dice (about ¼" cubes)
- 1 pound pork spare ribs
- ½ cup white wine
- 3 (28 ounce) cans tomato sauce, preferable san marzano tomatoes
- 1 tablespoon tomato paste, mixed with ¼ cup of water
- ¼ cup fresh basil leaves, whole

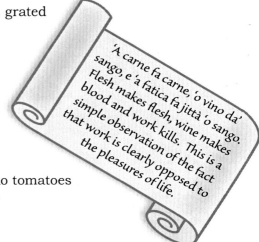

'A carne fa carne, 'o vino da' sango, e 'a fatica fa jittà 'o sango. Flesh makes flesh, wine makes blood and work kills. This is a simple observation of the fact that work is clearly opposed to the pleasures of life.

Directions:

1. Pound braciola and pork loin with a meat mallet. Lay individual slices of meat flat on a work surface and season with cheese, minced garlic, chopped parsley, and a pinch of salt and pepper. Roll each piece and tie with cooking twine.

2. Heat olive oil in a large pot, then add onion, rolled meat, and ribs and cook until meat is brown on all sides, about 10 minutes. Add white wine and mix with a wooden spoon. Cook for 2 minutes then add tomato sauce. Put ½ cup of water in each sauce can or bottle, swirl and add to pot. Add tomato paste mixture, fresh basil, and salt to taste. Bring to boil then lower heat and simmer partially covered with a lid for 2 ½ to 3 hours, stirring occasionally.

3. The result will be a thick and dark sauce that can be used to season a pasta of your choice, while the meat will serve as a main course.

Notes:

Alternately, substitute the pork loin or spare ribs with Italian sweet sausages and red wine for white wine.

Pasta, Potatoes, and Provola
Pasta, Patate, e Provola ('A past, patan, e provola)

```
Yields: 4 servings
Prep Time: 20 minutes
Cooking Time: 55 minutes
```

A dish loved by Neapolitans. *"Pasta, Patate, e Provola"* is a triple P magic formula, taking simple and inexpensive pantry ingredients and transforming them into utter deliciousness. *"Provola"* (smoked mozzarella) is an Italian cheese that originates from Campania and is made from cow's milk. Like most Neapolitan recipes, Pasta, Potatoes, and Provola, is one of the many delectable dishes that was once considered a poor peasant dish dating back to the 17th century. Today it is one of the most representative and appreciated Neapolitan dishes, with a truly unique and rustic flavor. Traditionally pork fat was used to sauté the vegetables but we substituted it with extra virgin olive oil. Another important ingredient is the grind of parmigiano, or cheese crust, which many discard after the meat of the cheese is gone, not knowing what they have lost. We add it to this dish, as well as many other recipes. As it cooks the crust becomes soft releasing part of the cheese still attached, transforming the dish into a delicacy of creaminess, while the outer part, carefully cleaned and grated, is chewed. We always fight over who will get the parmigiano grind but have come up with a solution. We cut it into pieces so that each person will have a small bite to enjoy. If you have never tried this dish before, get ready, your world is about to change! This is one of those dishes where the potatoes and pasta are cooked together, creating a well-defined flavor with each spoonful. This is an irresistible dish filled with happiness!

Ingredients:

- ½ cup extra virgin olive oil
- 1 garlic clove, minced
- ½ medium onion, small dice (about ¼" cubes)
- 3 stalks celery, small dice (about 1 cup)
- 4 plum tomatoes, small dice (about 2 cups)
- 3 to 4 leaves fresh basil, cut in half
- 1½ pounds potatoes (about 4 potatoes), peeled, cut into small dice, and submerged in juice and peel of one lemon and cold water to cover
- Parmigiano Reggiano grind (about 1½ by 3")
- 1 teaspoon sea salt
- 5 cups filtered water
- 8 ounces gluten-free mixed pasta (*pasta mista*)*
- 8 ounces provola (substitute with scamorza), small dice
- ½ cup freshly grated Parmigiano Reggiano cheese, to taste

Directions:

1. Heat oil in a Dutch oven, then add garlic and sauté for 2 minutes. Add onions, celery, tomato, and basil and cook for 5 minutes. Add potatoes, parmigiano grind, and salt, mix well and cook for 2 minutes. Add water and bring to a boil, then lower heat and simmer covered for 40 to 45 minutes, stirring occasionally, until potatoes are tender.
2. When potatoes are ready, add pasta and cook for 8 to 10 minutes. Turn off heat, add provola and mix well until the provola is completely melted.
3. Served hot topped with freshly grated Parmigiano Reggiano cheese and basil leaf as garnish.

Notes:

Eliminate bacon (or animal fat) to make it vegetarian.

Store leftovers in an airtight container refrigerated for two days.

*Alternately prepare your own mixed pasta with the following: elbow, mini penne, linguini, and fettuccini cut into smaller pieces.

Pasta and Beans
Tagliatelle e Fagioli (Taccun e fasul)

> Yields: 6 servings
> Prep Time: 45 minutes, plus 6 to 12 hours bean soaking time
> Cook Time: 30 minutes

"*Taccun e Fasul*," a historic and typical dish, born approximately 2,000 years ago. It is a remarkable ancient dish, which came primarily from the kitchens of farmers and farm laborers, with each region of Campania having its own version. It's one of those dishes where the pasta is cooked directly with the legumes instead of being cooked separately. In Naples it is typically made with cranberry beans and mixed pasta, known as "*munuzzaglia.*" Our family uses fresh cranberry beans, when available, but we make it mostly with cannellini beans creating a creamier sauce. At times my family adds "*le cotiche di mailae*" (pig skin) to the sauce to make the dish richer. Taccun e Fasul is a beloved dish and prepared with great joy, no matter which version you decide to use. We prepared ours with a homemade, gluten-free version of "*Taccun.*" Making homemade pasta always brings back memories of my grandmother Pasqualina, using the same board to make various pastas with her hands. A spectacular dish that warms the heart and stomach on slightly cold evenings, but can be enjoyed throughout the year!

Ingredients:

For beans

- 1 pound cannellini beans, soaked overnight, floating beans discarded, drained and rinsed*
- 1 bay leaf
- Pinch sea salt

For dough:

- 2 cups fine white rice flour, plus more for dusting
- 1 cup potato flour
- ½ cup of fine corn meal
- 2 eggs
- ½ teaspoon sea salt
- 1 ½ cups water
- 1-2 teaspoons of extra-virgin olive oil, as needed

For sauce:

- 28 ounces San Marzano whole peeled plum tomatoes (1 can)
- ¼ cup of extra virgin olive oil
- 2 ounces onion, thinly sliced
- 2 garlic cloves, peeled and whole
- 2 stalks celery, small diced (about 1 cup)
- ½ cup basil, chopped
- Sea salt and red crushed pepper to taste
- 4 cups cooked cannellini beans
- ¼ cup freshly grated Parmigiano Reggiano or pecorino Romano cheese

Directions:

For beans:

1. Transfer beans to a Dutch oven. Cover with water by 1 to 2 inches above the level of beans, add bay leaf and bring to a boil. Turn down heat and simmer covered for 1 ½ to 2 hours, stirring occasionally. When beans are cooked add salt and discard bay leaf.

For pasta dough:

2. Place a clean tablecloth on a flat surface and sprinkle with corn flour. In a large bowl combine rice flour, potato flour, and cornmeal. Make a well in the middle and add eggs, salt, and then water a little at a time. Begin mixing from the center with a fork and then with a wooden spoon or clean hands until a dough begins to form.

3. Turn dough onto a lightly floured surface and knead for 5 to 8 minutes or until you have a soft round ball (because this is gluten-free pasta dough, there is no gluten to stretch and "activate" but kneading ensures a smooth dough). If dough begins to stick to the wooden surface, spread 1 teaspoon of olive oil on the surface and knead as directed above.

4. Cut dough into four evenly sized pieces and shape each into a soft round ball. Sprinkle a wooden surface with flour and flatten each ball of dough with a rolling pin into a sheet approximately 10 by 7 inches and 1/8 inch thick. Place each sheet on the prepared table cloth, sprinkle with some corn flour and let it rest for about 1 hour.

5. With a chef's knife or pizza wheel, cut each sheet into vertical strips of about 1 inch wide. Dust one strip with flour and place a second strip on top. Cut stacked strips into approximately ¼ inch pieces, adding flour to prevent sticking. This will yield about 1 1/2 pounds of pasta. Place the cut pasta on the tablecloth, sprinkle with corn flour and let dry for approximately 3 to 4 hours or overnight. Cut any leftover uneven pieces into small squares and store in the freezer in an airtight container for 1 to 2 months. Add them to your favorite soups.

For Sauce:

6. Empty tomato can into a large bowl and crush tomatoes with your hands or pulse in a food processor for a few seconds. Set aside.

7. Heat oil in a large pot, then add garlic and onion and cook until onions begin to sweat and garlic turns a golden brown, about 4 to 5 minutes. Add crushed tomatoes, celery, basil, salt, and pepper and simmer for 10 minutes. Add cooked beans and simmer for another 30 minutes.

8. While sauce cooks bring cold water to boil in a large pot. Add pasta and cook for about 7 to 10 minutes. Drain and add to bean sauce. Mix well, turn off heat, and let it sit for 5 minutes.

9. Serve hot topped with freshly grated cheese.

Notes:

Do not store leftover beans in a glass container since beans tend to expand when frozen and they can shatter the glass.

Store pasta and beans in an airtight container refrigerated for one day.

From The Oven

"Dal Forno"

$\mathcal{T}$he term "Dal Forno" means "baked" in Italian and it is one of the most fantastic ways to prepare seriously superb comfort foods! My grandparents only had a "forno al legno" (wood-burning oven) where they cooked and baked everything including bread, pizza, potatoes, and desserts. The taste of food cooked in a wood oven is vastly different; there is something special and authentic about a wood-burning oven giving food an irresistible flavor with an unmistakable taste and aroma. These traditional family recipes I'm sharing with you were originally baked in a wood-burning oven and brought so much joy to the table.

Gattò di Patate (Potato Casserole)..42

Mamma's Pepperoni Imbottiti (Mamma's Stuffed Peppers)........................44

Parmigiana di Zucchine (Zucchini Parmigiana)..46

Tagliatelle Nidi di Uccelli (Baked Tagliatelle Birds Nest)...........................48

Potato Gateau (Casserole)
Gattò di Patate ('O gatto' 'e patan)

> Yields: 6 to 8 servings
> Prep Time: 30 minutes
> Cooking Time: 1 hour 10 minutes

A dangerous dish! Once you start you can't seem to stop!

This famous and ancient dish is a cornerstone of Neapolitan cuisine prepared with potatoes and various "*salumi*." What are salumi you ask? Good question! Salumi refers to cured meats and the word salume (plural is salumi) literally means "salted meats." Each family in the Campania region hands down their own version of this incredibly delicious creation. The traditional cultural heritage of the locals, especially in smaller rural towns, is to slaughter the pig themselves and use all of it so that nothing goes to waste. The use of pork, especially salted and processed into salumi, has immense ancient roots. According to historians, the origins of salumi can be traced back to the Etruscan and Roman times, although meat conservation practices can be traced back to more ancient times, even going back to the Paleolithic era.

This is one of our family favorites and is usually served as a first course, but can be served as a complete meal. The ingredients vary according to each region and personal taste. Our family recipe includes potatoes, eggs, soppressata, prosciutto, scamorza, pecorino, mozzarella, and breadcrumbs. This baked pie has a soft and creamy texture and is wrapped in a golden crispy crust that is mouthwatering right out of the oven. A dish difficult to resist making it perfect for a lunch or dinner with family and friends.

Ingredients:

- 4 pounds potatoes (about 5 large potatoes), peeled, cut in quarters
- 1 tablespoon sea salt, plus more to taste
- 2 ounces prosciutto (or ham), small diced (about ¼" cubes)
- 2 ounces soppressata (or salami), small diced
- 4 ounces mozzarella, small diced
- 2 ounces smoked scamorza, small diced (optional)
- 1 large egg
- ¼ cup freshly grated pecorino Romano or Parmigiano Reggiano cheese
- ¼ cup fresh parsley, chopped
- ½ teaspoon ground black pepper
- ½ cup gluten-free bread crumbs
- 1 tablespoons extra virgin olive oil, plus more for drizzling

Directions:

1. Preheat oven to 375°F.
2. Combine potatoes and 1 tablespoon salt in a large pot with enough water to cover. Bring to a boil, then simmer partially covered with a lid for 20 to 25 minutes until potatoes are fork-tender. Drain, peel, and pass through a potato ricer then set aside to cool.
3. In a large bowl, add prosciutto, soppressata, mozzarella, and scamorza. Add potatoes, egg, cheese, parsley, pepper and salt to taste. Mix until well combined.
4. Grease a 10 x 10 or 12 x 8 baking dish with olive oil. Add the mixture to the dish and flatten with wet fingers. Top with bread crumbs and then drizzle with olive oil. Bake for 45 minutes until top is a golden brown. Allow to rest for 15 minutes before serving.
5. Cut into squares and serve.

Notes:

If potatoes are too floury, dilute with a small amount of milk.

This dish can be prepared a few days before and stored with double plastic wrap in the refrigerator. Simply heat the oven and bake.

Mamma's Stuffed Peppers
Mamma's Pepperoni Imbottiti ('E puparuole 'mbuttite)

Yields: 12 stuffed peppers
Prep Time: 45 minutes, plus 15 minutes for roasting peppers
Cook Time: 1 hour

A dish that my mamma has prepared for as long as I can remember. This is a recipe packed with glorious Mediterranean flavors and one that is known in the Neapolitan dialect as *"puparuoli 'mbuttunat"* - rich, substantial, and thoroughly delicious! Stuffed peppers and its existing variations are a must in southern Italy. It is a dish that was once considered a poor food because it did not include rice or pasta for the filling. Rice was a dish for the rich and impossible to buy for the less fortunate. Instead, many filled their peppers with intelligently recycled leftovers such as stale bread, anchovies, capers, and anything else that was available in the fridge. In Naples, popular cuisine is creative cuisine always looking for new ways to avoid waste but in a tasty way. As they say, *"a buttare il cibo e' sempre un peccato"*, meaning "throwing away food is always a sin," representing a thrifty and humble culture of the Neapolitan people. My mamma uses red peppers as she likes them best. Feel free to use orange or yellow peppers as well. It is considered a summer dish that can be served as a first or second course meal.

Ingredients:

- 12 red bell peppers, roasted and cleaned
- 7 ounces prosciutto cotto (or ham), small diced (about ¼" cubes)
- 4 ½ ounces soppressata (or salami), small diced
- 30 ounces smoked scamorza, small diced
- 4 ounces mozzarella (125 g), small dice
- 3 ounces freshly grated Parmigiano Reggiano cheese
- ¼ cup parsley, chopped
- ½ teaspoon ground black pepper
- 3 eggs plus 1 egg white, lightly beaten together
- ¼ cup extra virgin olive oil, plus more for drizzling
- 2 to 3 cups gluten-free bread crumbs

Directions:

1. Preheat oven to 350°F. Prepare a large ceramic baking pan by adding olive oil to lightly cover the bottom. Set aside.
2. Cook whole peppers directly on the burner of a gas stove over high heat. Roast peppers until skin is blackened on all sides, using tongs to turn as needed, about 15 minutes. Once fully charred, transfer peppers to a large glass bowl and cover with a kitchen towel or in a brown paper bag. Allow to cool for 15 minutes.
3. While peppers are cooling, add prosciutto, soppressata, scamorza, mozzarella, Parmigiano, parsley and pepper in a large bowl. Add beaten eggs and mix with a fork or rubber spatula. Set aside.

4. Once peppers are cool enough to handle, use a paring knife to cut off the tops of the peppers and remove the charred black skin. You can keep the shape of the pepper whole, or you can cut a slit down each pepper lengthwise, open it, clean out the seeds and charred layer, then fold the pepper closed. Keep a small bowl of water nearby for keeping your hands clean. Do not rinse peppers under water. Discard black layer along with stem and seeds. Transfer peppers to a clean glass bowl.

5. Create an assembly in your kitchen space or table beginning with the peppers, mixture of salumi and cheese, breadcrumbs, and baking pan. Place a pepper in one of your hands. Stuff 2 tablespoons of the salumi/cheese filling inside the pepper. If the pepper is cut on one side, use your hands to close the edges shut. Cover top with a few tablespoons of bread crumbs. Place peppers upright in prepared baking pan. Repeat with remaining peppers, tightly fitting in the pan.

6. Drizzle olive oil on top of the peppers and bake until golden brown on top, about 1 hour.

Notes:

Traditionally, this recipe calls for anchovies so feel free to add them to the mix.

Bakes stuffed peppers can be stored in the refrigerator and consumed within 4 days.

Prior to baking, stuffed peppers can be frozen in an airtight container for up to 4 weeks.

You can store roasted (unstuffed) peppers, covered with plastic, and refrigerated for a week.

For our vegetarian friends, make a savory rice filling. Sauté minced garlic and quartered cherry tomatoes in a large sauté pan with a bit of olive oil. Add small diced vegetables (your choice), cooked rice, sliced black olives, and capers. (You will need 1½ cups filling). Stuff peppers and cook as written above, reducing the bake time to 40 minutes.

If extra salumi and cheese mixture remains, add eggs and make a frittata!

Zucchini Parmigiana
Parmigiana di Zucchine ('A parmiggian e cucuzziell)

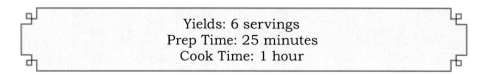

Yields: 6 servings
Prep Time: 25 minutes
Cook Time: 1 hour

"*Parmigiana di Zucchine*" is a different way of preparing the classic "*Parmigiana di Melanzane,*" or eggplant parmigiana, as we know it in the United States and around the world. Historians say that Parmigiana di Melanzane has been around since the 1700's, however there are several controversial issues as to the origin of this famous dish. Regardless of the origin, it is an incredibly tasty dish with recipes having different variations from one region to another. We enjoy preparing this classic dish with zucchini, which is also a popular alternative of this fantastic Mediterranean recipe. Zucchini Parmigiana is perfect as an appetizer, first, or second dish. The choice is yours! The authentic flavors produce a unique result that will intoxicate your taste buds. This dish will be a favorite amongst everyone and it is even better the next day. The result is always a perfect combination of summertime flavors and a dish to be enjoyed hot, fresh from the oven, or lukewarm on summer evenings.

Ingredients:

- 2½ pounds medium zucchini (about 3), sliced lengthwise
- 3 Eggs
- Pinch of sea salt, plus more to taste
- ¼ cup water
- 1 cup organic sunflower or vegetable oil
- 1 cup one-to-one gluten free flour
- 6 ounces fresh mozzarella, shredded
- 1 cup freshly grated Parmigiano Reggiano or pecorino Romano, plus more for garnish
- Ground black pepper to taste

For Sauce:

- ¼ cup extra virgin olive oil
- 2 garlic cloves, whole
- ½ small onion, small diced (about ¼" cubes)
- 2 (24 ounce) cans tomato purée
- 5 to 6 basil leaves, whole
- Sea salt to taste

Directions:

1. Line a baking sheet with a clean kitchen towel or paper towels.
2. Using a mandolin, slice lengthwise approximately 1/8 inch thick and place on prepared baking sheet covering each layer with paper towels. Set aside to dry for 1 to 2 hours.

For sauce:

3. Heat oil in a large pot, then add garlic, and onion and cook until onions begin to sweat and garlic turns a golden brown, about 4 to 5 minutes. Add tomato puree, basil, and salt to taste and simmer for 30 minutes.

For zucchini:

4. While sauce cooks, add eggs, pinch of salt, and water in a bowl and mix well with a fork. In a separate bowl, add flour. Dip each zucchini slice in flour, shaking off excess flour and set aside.
5. Heat oil in a large high-sided sauté pan. Place a paper-towel lined baking sheet tray next to the pan, fry all the zucchini until golden brown, about 2 minutes on each side and place in the prepared baking sheet, adding additional paper towels after each layer.

To bake:

6. Preheat oven to 350°F.
7. To assemble the dish, coat the bottom of a rectangular baking dish with sauce and arrange zucchini in an even layer over the tomato sauce, alternating horizontally and then vertically, in a lattice design to keep everything in place. Sprinkle each layer with some mozzarella, ¼ cup Parmigiano Reggiano cheese and a ladle of tomato sauce. Proceed alternating layers until all zucchini is used. Top the last layer with remaining sauce, mozzarella, and a good amount of Parmigiano Reggiano then bake for 30 to 35 minutes, until bubbling and browned on top and edges. Remove from heat and allow to sit for 5 minutes.
8. Garnish with grated Parmigiano Reggiano cheese before serving.

Notes:

An alternative to Parmigiana di Zucchini is to make it a white parmigiana. Simply remove the sauce and add extra cheese.

To bake instead of frying, after flouring zucchini, place them on a parchment-lined baking sheet, drizzle zucchini with extra virgin olive oil, and bake at 350°F for 15 to 20 minutes, until lightly browned, turning zucchini halfway through so that all sides bake evenly.

Baked Tagliatelle Birds Nests
Tagliatelle Nidi di Uccelli ('E nid d'auciell)

Yields: 8 servings
Prep Time: 1 hour
Cook Time: 1 hour

These nests made from fresh tagliatelle are easy to make and versatile. They are suitable for all occasions and a fantastic dish when you have guests and want to amaze them with a beautiful presentation! This is a recipe that my mamma Giovanna learned from her cousin Giovanna. These delightful little nests are an alternative way to prepare tagliatelle. A few ingredients allow you to create a dough to form different shaped pastas. The nests are created with fresh tagliatelle and twirled with your fingers to create a small nest and then left to dry so that the pasta remains intact. The nests must be fully dried before placing them in a baking pan and then filled and topped before placing them in the oven to be baked. You do not pre-cook these nests. The cooking of pasta takes place in the oven and that is why the nests should be completely covered with the sauce.

Different variations can be used for the filling and sauce. All you need is your imagination! Create the combinations you prefer to obtain a tasty dish. For this recipe we used a gluten-free version for fresh pasta dough and our traditional and classic ragù sauce. If you are pressed for time and want to use store bought gluten-free, this shaped pasta can be found in specialty stores and various supermarkets.

Ingredients:

For tagliatelle:
- 2 cups fine white rice flour, plus more for dusting
- 1 cup potato flour
- ½ cup cornmeal
- 2 eggs
- ½ teaspoon salt
- 1 ½ cups water
- 1-2 teaspoons of extra-virgin olive oil, as needed

For meat:
- 1 ½ pounds mixed chopped meat (veal, pork, and beef)
- ¼ cup extra virgin olive oil
- 1 medium onion, thinly sliced

- 2 cups shredded mozzarella
- ¼ teaspoon ground black pepper
- ½ teaspoon sea salt
- 2 eggs
- For tomato sauce:
- ¼ cup extra virgin olive oil
- ½ small onion, small diced (about ¼" cubes)
- 2 garlic cloves, whole
- 2 (24-ounce) cans tomato purée
- 5 to 6 basil leaves

For assembly:
- ½ cup freshly grated Parmigiano Reggiano or pecorino Romano, to taste

Directions:

For homemade pasta, to be prepared the day before:*
1. In a bowl, use a fork to mix fine white rice flour, potato flour and cornmeal. Make a well in the middle and add eggs, salt and water a little at a time. Begin mixing from the center with fork and then your hands until a dough begins to form.

2. Turn dough onto a rice flour-dusted surface and knead for 5 to 8 minutes or until you have a soft, round dough. Because this is a gluten-free pasta dough, there is no gluten to stretch and "activate", but kneading ensures a smooth dough with no flour clumps. If dough begins to stick to the wooden surface, add 1 teaspoon of olive oil and spread on the surface and continue kneading.

3. Cut dough into 4 evenly-sized pieces, and slightly flatten each piece with your fingers. Using a pasta machine, pass each piece of dough through the flat attachment, 2 to 3 times, folding the dough each time before passing through, until you have a smooth, clean pasta sheet. Cut off the ends to make a perfect sheet and set aside. Do the same for the remaining pieces of dough. If dough sticks, add additional flour.

4. Prepare a baking sheet with a clean kitchen towel and some rice flour. Pass each sheet through the tagliatelle pasta attachment and create the nests by placing them in a circle from above to create a perfect nest with a hollow center for the filling. Top the nests with a sprinkle of rice flour. The pasta will need to dry completely before baking it in the oven. Prepare the pasta ahead of time as it may take 1 to 2 days to fully dry.

For meat:

5. In a mixing bowl, add mixed meats and combine well with a wooden spoon. Set aside.

6. Heat olive oil in a deep-sided frying pan and add onions. Sauté over medium heat until onions are translucent. Add mixed chopped meat to the pan and mix well. Keep turning meat until browned and oil has been absorbed, about 5 minutes.

7. Remove from heat and place the mixture in a large glass mixing bowl. Add mozzarella, pepper, salt and mix well. Set aside to cool. Once the mixture has cooled, add eggs and mix well with your hands.

For tomato sauce:

8. In a large pot, add olive oil, onion and garlic. Sauté over medium heat until onion is translucent, about 2 to 3 minutes.

9. Add tomato purée and basil and simmer for 30 minutes. Raise heat to bring tomato sauce to a boil. It must be boiling before adding it to the baking tray with tagliatelle nests.

To finish:

10. Preheat oven to 400°F.

11. Use a ladle to cover the bottom of a large baking dish with tomato sauce. Place tagliatelle nests close together over sauce. Add a tablespoon of the meat mixture to each tagliatelle nest. If there is any leftover mixture, divide among the nests. Cover each nest with boiling-hot tomato sauce. (The heat of the sauce plus the oven will cook the pasta.) You should have enough tomato sauce in the baking dish to cover a little more than half of the nests. Top with pecorino Romano or Parmigiano Reggiano cheese.

12. Cover with foil and bake for 20 minutes. Remove foil and return to oven, uncovered, for another 20 minutes until deeply golden on top.

Notes:

You can always substitute with store-bought marinara sauce if desired.

You can use the fresh sheets of pasta to make gluten-free lasagna.

For our vegetarian friends, you can use your choice of vegetarian cheese and add vegetables to the sauce. Small diced onions, carrots, zucchini, eggplant, and/or mushrooms; cooked in tomato sauce for about 10 minutes.

To store fresh pasta: Line baking sheet with a clean kitchen towel. Dust towel with rice flour and place the pasta on top. Store in freezer for one hour then transfer pasta to a freezer bag and store for up to 6 weeks.

*Substitute fresh pasta with gluten-free fettuccini already dried and packaged as a nest.

Meat Dishes

"La Carne"

*T*he Campania region is known for its beautiful ocean, landscapes, nutrient-rich soils and many culinary traditions that continue to exist today. Inland of the Campania there is an abundant amount of land available for livestock making meat dishes more common. Lamb, pork, veal, rabbit, and poultry are often used in recipes. For many centuries Campania has been home to the native water buffalo. From buffalo milk comes the ever amazing buffalo mozzarella and incredibly delicious ice-cream!

Goat with Peas, Cacio (cheese) and Eggs (Capretto, Cacio, ed Uova) 54

Mamma's Meatballs (Polpette di Mamma) 56

Mamma's Traditional Roasted Lamb with Potatoes 58
   (Agnello al Forno con Patate di Mamma)

Pork with Potatoes and Papaccelle 60
   (Costolette di Mailae con Patate e Papaccelle)

Sausage and Friarielli (Salsiccia e Friarielli)..62

Goat with Peas, Cacio and Eggs
Capretto, Cacio, ed Uova (O' capretto cu 'e pesielle caso e ove)

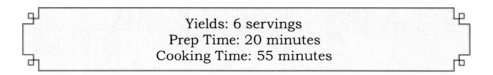

Yields: 6 servings
Prep Time: 20 minutes
Cooking Time: 55 minutes

Goat with peas, "*cacio*" (cheese), and eggs is an unforgettable, mouthwatering and unique dish of the Neapolitan tables that is substantial and truly welcoming; a pairing that is so divine that you'll want to eat it throughout the year! It is known as a dish of ancient origins whose typical preparation has been handed down from generation to generation. "*Capretto, Cacio, ed Uova*" is filled with rustic flavors with the strong taste of kid (goat) expertly dampened by the most fragrant aromatic herbs. As with most Easter dishes, this too has a symbolic ingredient - the eggs. In fact, eggs are considered the symbol of life and rebirth.

This classic, rich and hearty dish is loved and enjoyed by all. Tasting is believing!

Ingredients:

- 3 pounds goat (substitute with lamb), large diced (about 1" cubes)
- 1/3 cup extra virgin olive oil
- 1 large onion, small diced (about ¼" cubes)
- 2 sprigs of fresh rosemary, chopped, plus full sprigs for garnish
- ½ cup white wine
- 2 pounds freshly shelled peas
- 1 cup of water
- 4 eggs
- ½ cup freshly grated Parmigiano Reggiano or pecorino Romano, plus more for topping
- ½ teaspoon sea salt
- ½ teaspoon ground black pepper

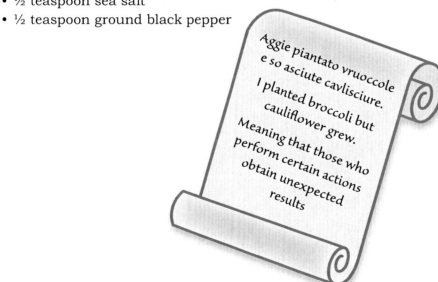

Aggie piantato vruoccole e so asciute cavlisciure.

I planted broccoli but cauliflower grew.

Meaning that those who perform certain actions obtain unexpected results

Directions:

1. Marinate meat overnight with water, lemon, wine, and fresh herbs. Pat meat with a paper towel to dry before frying.
2. Heat oil in a large high-sided non-stick sauté pan, add meat and gently turn until all sides are brown, about 10 minutes. Turn down heat and add onion and rosemary and mix well. Gradually add white wine, and cook for another 10 minutes allowing wine to evaporate. Add peas and water and mix together until well combined. Reduce heat and simmer for 15 to 20 minutes, covered, until peas are tender.
3. Meanwhile, in a large bowl, add eggs, cheese, salt, and black pepper and mix well with a fork. Pour mixture over the meat and cook for another 5 minutes, while continually stirring. If too dry, add ¼ of water.
4. Sprinkle with freshly grated cheese and serve with a sprig of rosemary as garnish.

Notes:

Alternately, use zucchini cut into large cubes as a substitute for meat.

Mamma's Meatballs
Polpette di Mamma (Purpett e' mamma')

```
Yields: 30-35 meatballs
Prep Time: 20 minutes
Bake Time: 35 to 40 minutes
```

Neapolitan meatballs are an ancient preparation handed down by our grandmothers, also known as the"*polpette*" queens! Polpette and sauce is among the oldest and most renowned dishes of the Neapolitan culinary tradition with the polpette usually served as a "*secondo piatto*" (second dish). This is a dish that is appreciated and loved by the entire family, especially our little nieces and nephews! Our family has become extremely creative when it comes to inventing different versions of this classic dish. This is a recipe I grew up with that is traditionally made with old hardened bread crumbs. For the gluten-free version, we made gluten-free Italian bread and stored the crumbs in the freezer until ready to use.

On Sunday mornings, these little delicacies release a delicious aroma that permeates throughout the entire house. It is a miracle that there are enough meatballs left to add to the sauce since we all tend to sneak in and grab a few while they are cooking. Even our dog Franklyn participated, however his meatballs would somehow miraculously fall out of the frying pan and onto the floor for him to enjoy. When asked, my mamma would always say that it slipped right out of the frying pan while turning them. Really? That never, ever happened before, but somehow always seemed to happen when Franklyn was around. I get it though - he was irresistible and so were the meatballs!!! We would all get scolded for eating them, except Franklyn, of course.

Meatballs are a convenient dish because the sauce is used to season the pasta and we have the pleasure of cleaning the plate with bread known as "*scarpetta*" (shoe), so that we had a clean plate for the "*polpette.*" In Italy my mamma made the meatballs with scraps of pork and beef. Veal was not used because it was extremely expensive so they would use additional bread instead. Traditional meatballs are fried and adding fried meatballs to the sauce is even better. However, in my quest to keep my family somewhat healthy during our Sunday lunch gatherings, I decided to bake them and discovered that some of us, who shall remain nameless, prefer baked polpette instead of the fried version. Yup, it's true! However, if you prefer cooking them the traditional way, directions were added under the "Notes" section. One thing is for sure, they do not fail to delight the palate and no one ever says no to polpette. Polpette can be served as an amazing second dish or make smaller ones to accompany an aperitif! Deliciousness all in under an hour!

Ingredients:

- 1 ½ to 2 pounds mix of ground veal, pork, and beef
- 1 pound gluten-free bread, crust removed (about 1 3/4 cups)*
- ½ cup fresh parsley, chopped
- 1 garlic clove, minced

- 1 cup of pecorino Romano or Parmigiano Reggiano cheese, grated
- 4 eggs
- Sea salt to taste
- Ground black pepper to taste
- Fresh parsley as garnish

Directions:

1. In a mixing bowl, combine ground meat together.
2. Using your hands, crumble the soft part of the bread and cut the crust into small (1/8 to 1/4 inch) cubes.
3. In a large mixing bowl, add ground meat, bread mixture, parsley, garlic, cheese, eggs, salt and pepper. Work the mixture with your hands to combine all ingredients well, about 15 minutes.
4. Preheat oven to 350°F.
5. Line a large baking sheet with parchment paper. Shape meatballs into 1 ½" balls and place on prepared baking sheet. Bake for 35 to 40 minutes.**
6. Garnish with sprigs of fresh parsley.

Notes:

Add cooked meatballs to a tomato sauce and simmer for another 10 to 15 minutes to absorb the flavors of the sauce.

Store leftover meatballs in an airtight container refrigerated for two days. Or freeze for two to three months.

*Substituting with breadcrumbs is not recommended as it will result in dry polpette.

**To fry meatballs: Heat 1½ cups organic cold-pressed canola or vegetable oil in a high-sided sauté pan. Place a paper-towel lined baking sheet tray next to pot. When oil is hot, add meatballs a few at a time, leaving at least two inches of space around each one so as not to crowd the pan. Gently turn with a fork or tongs until all sides are evenly browned, about 10 to 15 minutes then transfer to towel-lined tray to drain.

Mamma's Roasted Lamb with Potatoes
Mamma's Agnello al Forno con Patate (Agnello 'o furn 'cu e' patane)

> Yields: 6 servings
> Prep time: 30 to 40 minutes
> Cooking Time: 1 hour 30 minutes

This perfect combination of lamb and potatoes is a typical Easter dish and one that can be enjoyed throughout the year, especially during our classic Sunday family gatherings. The most devoted to traditions will not fail to bring a typical lamb dish to the Easter table. The lamb brings with it Christian suggestions and symbols still alive and honored and it is by far the most significant Easter symbol. The lamb is said to be the symbol of sacrifice and it is for this reason that the lamb is brought to the table on Easter. It also represents the Resurrection of Jesus, a new beginning that embodies purity and goodness. Lamb's unmistakable taste of wild notes, make it a unique and much loved Easter dish. Baked lamb with potatoes is a simple and rustic recipe that my mamma has prepared for many years and is loved by all, especially her brothers! The lamb is flavored with fragrant aromas that soften its pungent taste and baking it in the oven will return a tender and juicy meat. We use the potato-base as a sauce with pasta and serve it as a "*primo piatto*" (first course) and the lamb is served as the "*secondo piatto*" (second course). It is one of the most delicious ways to eat lamb.

As with so many other recipes, I followed my mamma with pen and paper trying to decipher measurements. When it came to parmigiano, I inquired as to the amount of cheese she was adding to the pan. Mamma's response was, "*una bella mangiata e' parmigiano.*" My response, "that's lovely mom but: 1) How do you even translate that into English? and 2) How do I translate that into cups"? It basically means, use a fistful or a good amount of parmigiano! To make this delectable dish gluten-free, simply substitute with gluten-free pasta.

Ingredients:

For marinade:

- 5 pounds bone-in leg of lamb, cut into equal sizes (about 1" pieces) (substitute with lamb shanks)
- 2 cups red wine
- ¼ cup fresh rosemary, chopped
- ¼ cup fresh sage, chopped
- ½ teaspoon sea salt
- ¼ teaspoon black ground pepper

For roast:

- ¾ cups extra virgin olive oil
- 2 ½ pounds Russet potatoes, washed, cut into large dice (about ¾"), and rinsed to remove excess starch
- 3 plum tomatoes, large diced
- 1 medium onion, sliced
- 1 pound fresh or frozen peas
- ½ cup fresh parsley, chopped
- ½ cup freshly grated Parmigiano Reggiano cheese
- Sea salt and ground black pepper to taste
- 2 cups water

Directions:

1. To marinate the lamb: In a large bowl, place the lamb, red wine, and fresh herbs. Add salt and pepper to taste and mix to coat. Cover and refrigerate for one hour.
2. Preheat oven to 350°F.
3. Heat oil in a large round pan over medium-high heat. Add lamb and cook for 8 to 10 minutes on each side until browned. Add potatoes, tomatoes, onions, peas, parsley, Parmigiano, salt and pepper.
4. Add water to the pan; it should be level with, but not covering, the meat. Bring water to a boil, then stir with a wooden spoon and transfer the pan to the oven. Bake for 1½ to 2 hours, or until meat is tender.
5. Serve in a large platter and garnish with fresh sprigs of rosemary.

Notes:

To eliminate the strong taste of lamb, soak the lamb overnight in a solution of water and lemon.

Store leftovers in an airtight container and refrigerated, for 2 days. Reheat in the oven.

Pork with Potatoes and Papacelle

Costolette di Mailae con Patate e Papaccelle
(A carne 'e puorco cu 'e patan e papaccelle)

Yields: 6 servings
Prep Time: 15 minutes
Cook Time: 25 minutes

Pork with potatoes and *"papacelle"* is a tasty, unique and comforting dish that is sure to bring happiness into your home and belly, as only those recipes of tradition can. This recipe originates from my mamma's town of Durazzano and is one full of flavor, simple ingredients and is a beloved recipe of the Campania cuisine.

Papaccelle are small round-shaped peppers traditionally used for this dish. When preserved they are known as *"papaccelle sott'aceto,"* which literally means papaccelle under vinegar or pickled papaccelle. These delicious little peppers are famous when making the incredible *"Insalata di Baccala"* (Cod Fish Salad), as well as the typical *"L'insalata di Rinforzo"* (Reinforcement Salad). Since we are all huge fans of this dish, we make pork with potatoes and papacelle throughout the year. Foods are seasonal in Italy and papacelle peppers are available at the local markets from August through October. Neapolitan papaccelle are a smaller, fleshy, roundish and sweet-tasting type of pepper. They are excellent stuffed! In the United States they are difficult to find so when we visit the farmers markets and find them, we stock up, prepare, and store them. Whether here or in Italy, I enjoy shopping with my family at the outdoor markets. It is always a memorable and educational experience, chatting with the local farmers about seasonal and sustainable fruits and vegetables. Sometimes, when shopping on my own and unsure of the quality of a particular fruit or vegetable, I'll take pictures and text my family for guidance. My family members in both countries make sure I'm purchasing the best product by educating me on the what the produce should look and smell like. For this recipe we substituted papaccelle peppers with regular peppers, which are easier to find. You can use pickled peppers, which then eliminates the additional vinegar or simply follow our recipe below.

Ingredients:

- 2 ½ pounds papaccelle sott'aceto (substitute red and green bell peppers), sliced into strips
- 2 cups cold-pressed canola or vegetable oil
- 1 garlic clove, halved
- Salt to taste
- 2 ½ pounds potatoes, peeled, cut into ¾ inch pieces, and submerged in cold water to cover
- 1 ¾ pound pork loin, cut into evenly sized pieces (about 1")
- Crushed red pepper to taste
- ¼ cup red wine vinegar.

Directions:

1. If using fresh bell peppers, core, deseed and cut into long thin strips.
2. Heat oil in a large high sided sauté pan. When the oil is hot add garlic and let it cook for a minute then add potatoes and a pinch of salt. Cook on medium heat until potatoes are golden and crusty underneath, about 4 to 5 minutes. Gently flip potatoes and cook until golden on all sides. Continue flipping until potatoes are golden and crusty. Lift potatoes out of pan with a spider strainer and transfer to a large bowl. Carefully pour off excess oil leaving enough oil in pan to sauté peppers with.
3. Add peppers to hot pan and sauté, stirring often until peppers are soft, about 10 minutes. Add peppers to cooked potatoes.
4. In the same pan add about 1 tablespoon of oil, add pork pieces, crushed red pepper, and cook 4 to 5 minutes on each side. When cooked, add to potatoes and peppers. Add red wine vinegar and salt to taste. Mix well and serve!

Notes:

Alternatively, toss potatoes and peppers with olive oil and salt and spread on a parchment lined baking sheet. Bake in a 350°F oven for 25 to 30 minutes.

If you are lucky enough to find these delicious little masterpieces known as *"papacelle"* peppers, below is how you would clean and preserve them:

- It is essential that the papaccelle are very fresh, fleshy, and without any bruising since the vinegar will make them softer as time passes.
- Have a glass container, with a tight lid (already sterilized) ready. The size of the bottle depends on the amount of peppers you'd like to preserve.
- Wash the *papaccelle* and use a dish towel to dry each pepper. The pepper should remain intact, including the stalk, and no trace of wet or damp areas should be visible.
- Pour red wine vinegar into a sauce pot with a pinch of salt and bring to a boil.
- In the meantime, place the *papacelle* closely together in the glass container, being careful not to tear them. Pour the vinegar, little by little, over the *papacelle* and fill the container to the brim. Let the *papacelle* rest without covering. As time passes the vinegar level will settle. Top it off with more vinegar making sure that the topmost *papacelle* are covered. Keep uncovered overnight before sealing tightly and storing in a cool and dry place for twenty days. Use within 3 months.

Sausage and Friarielli

Salsiccia e Friarielli (Sasicc e friariell)

Yields: 4 servings
Prep Time: 20 minutes
Cooking Time: 40 minutes

"*Salsiccia e Friarielli*"(broccoli rabe) is a unique, simple, tasty and classic dish of the Neapolitan cuisine. The "*friarielli*" are a typical vegetable of the Campania region, rustic and full of character, whose origins can be traced back to the end of the 17th century. This bitter leafy green vegetable, rich in vitamins and minerals, is difficult to find outside of Italy and goes by different names. The Romans call it "*broccoletti*" due to its resemblance to broccoli and in Puglia they refer to it as "*cime di rapa.*" In the United States it is known as "*broccoli rabe.*" We used fresh broccoli rabe from the garden for this recipe. Broccoli rabe are fantastic on their own but moreso if cooked with sausages! Sausage and friarielli is a truly happy union that must be tried at least once in your life!

Ingredients:

- 4 bunches of friarielli (broccoli rabe)
- 8 pork sausages
- 1 tablespoon extra virgin olive oil, plus ½ cup
- ½ cup white wine
- 1 garlic clove, cut in half
- Pinch crushed red pepper
- Sea salt to taste

Homemade Sausages

Directions:

1. Remove the tender leaves and buds from the tougher stalks and wash under running cold water. Set aside in a colander.
2. Place sausages in a large high-sided sauté pan with a little water (about 2 tablespoons) and cook for 10 minutes.
3. Place the sausages in a non-stick pan with a little water and cook for about 10 minutes. Remove sausages from pan and pierce with prongs of a fork to remove excess water.* In the same pan add 1 tablespoon of oil, add sausages, and cook for 2 to 4 minutes. Add white wine and cook to brown for another 10 minutes.
4. Heat ½ cup oil in a large sauté pan, then add garlic and pepper and sauté for 1 to 2 minutes. Add friarielli and salt, and cook covered on a high heat for a few minutes, until friarielli are soft, then remove the lid and cook for 5 to 10 minutes more. Add sausages and cook on medium heat for another 5 minutes.
5. Place sausages on a bed of friarielli in the center of a serving dish and serve while hot!

Notes:

To remove some of the bitterness, blanch the friarielli in boiling water for 2 minutes before sautéing them.

**Piercing sausages releases the fat and makes them a little harder. Avoid piercing for softer sausages.*

Fish Dishes

"Pesce"

*I*n a seaside city like Naples, numerous fish markets crowd the city neighborhoods. Fish is the most loved cuisine by Neapolitans because of the heavy presence of freshly caught fish. The seafood markets are beautiful, colorful, and busy offering an amazing selection of fish to the locals. Known as the Mediterranean cuisine, seafood makes up the majority of the coastal diet, along with sun-kissed vegetables and fruits. The Campania region has access to many ports for fresh seafood, where fishermen still make a living from fishing along the coast. Fishermen return with carts of seafood such as squid, octopus, and sardines; where lively fish markets crowd the neighborhoods of the city, attesting to the region's reputation of having the best and most delectable seafood.

Peppered Mussels (Impepata di Cozze) 66
Poached Octopus (Polipetti Affogati) 68
Seafood Risotto (Risotto al Pescatore) 70

Peppered Mussels
Impepata di Cozze ('A'mpepat 'e cozz)

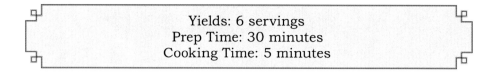

> Yields: 6 servings
> Prep Time: 30 minutes
> Cooking Time: 5 minutes

Peppered mussels are an absolute favorite of the family and a famous dish that is a cornerstone of the Neapolitan cuisine, a symbol of the magnificence of this seaside city. It is a perfect dish that represents the very essence of summer and eating it is like a ritual! Peppered mussels is a simple dish with a strong traditional connotation, eaten with pleasure especially during the summer months. *"Impepata di Cozze"* is a classic preparation typically served as an appetizer but we enjoy it as a main meal. In Naples it is still found on food carts at the port. This is a magnificent dish which will allow you to savor all of the flavors of a simple yet refined seafood dish. Impepata di Cozze are best enjoyed when accompanied by classic *"friselle"* or toasted bread and a nice glass of Italian white!

Ingredients:

- 4 pounds fresh mussels
- 3 tablespoons extra virgin olive oil
- 3 garlic cloves, thinly sliced*
- Pinch crushed red pepper
- 1 pound plum tomatoes, large diced (about 1" cubes)
- 2/4 cup fresh parsley, chopped and separated, plus more for garnish
- Pinch of sea salt
- Ground black pepper to taste
- Toasted gluten-free bread brushed with a garlic clove
- Lemon wedges as garnish

"Fa chiu' miracule o' vino ca Sant' Antonino."

Wine creates more miracles than Saint Anthony.

Directions:

1. Discard any mussels that are chipped, broken, damaged or open. Soak mussels in cold water and salt for 30 minutes to an hour. Remove one-by-one from the water, rinse under running water and set aside.

2. Heat oil in a large high-sided sauté pan, then add red pepper and garlic and sauté until garlic is golden brown. Add tomatoes, parsley, and salt and mix well. Cook covered until tomatoes are soft, about 5 minutes. Add mussels and cook covered on a low flame for 3 to 4 minutes. Add ¼ cup of parsley and cook for another 2 to 3 minutes. Uncover and as mussels begin opening, add a generous amount of pepper and ¼ cup of parsley. Cook for a few minutes more.

3. Discard mussels that are still closed and serve mussels in their own stock. Garnish with finely chopped parsley and lemon wedges.

Notes:

With this recipe you can make spaghetti with mussels. Simply cook the pasta, drain and return to pot. Add some juice from the mussels, stir, and place pasta in a bowl topped with mussels, additional juice, and chopped parsley.

*If you prefer to discard garlic after cooking, leave cloves whole.

Poached Octopus
Polipetti Affogati ('E purpetielle affugate)

Yields: 4 servings
Prep Time: 25 minutes
Cook Time: 40 to 50 minutes

According to historians, *"Polipetti Affogati"* was born in Borgo Santa Lucia, Naples where a group of fisherman created this exceptional dish destined to remain in the history of the Neapolitan cuisine. When in Naples this is a must! The secret to enjoying this true delicacy is that the octopus should cook in its own juices. *"Polipetti affogati"* literally means to *"affogare,"* or drown in tomato sauce and its own juices. When cooked the octopus releases liquids that flavor it during cooking. Poached octopus is a simple, fragrant and characteristic dish full of culinary art that has been passed down from generation to generation. Growing up in an Italian family, I can honestly say that our grandparents and parents had a way of simplifying things in the kitchen and turning that simplicity into something amazing. All they needed was imagination, creativity, and above all, practicality to create recipes that required little time but great passion.

Of course, we cannot forget the grand finale, *"La Scarpetta"* for the delicious sauce that is left after all the octopus is gone! La Scarpetta means *"to make a shoe,"* referring to using small pieces of bread to mop up the last of the sauce on your plate. Poached octopus is delicious as an appetizer or as a second dish to be enjoyed with toasted rustic bread or as a condiment for pasta.

Ingredients:

- 1/3 cup extra virgin olive oil
- 2 garlic cloves, thinly sliced
- Pinch of crushed red pepper (optional)
- 1 pint cherry tomatoes, cut in half
- ¼ cup fresh parsley, chopped, plus more for garnish
- ½ teaspoon sea salt
- ½ cup tomato sauce
- 2 pounds fresh baby octopus, cleaned, washed and dried*

"'O purpo se coce dint' all'acqua soja."

Octopus cooks in its own juces.

Meaning that things, people, or difficult events mature and resolve themselves over time.

Directions:

1. Heat oil in a five to six-quart Dutch oven, add garlic and red pepper and sauté for 1 minute, without letting the garlic brown. Add tomatoes, parsley and salt. Mix well and cook for 5 minutes, add tomato sauce and cook for 5 minutes more, then add octopus and cook covered for 25 to 30 minutes, or until tender. The octopus releases liquid while cooking.
2. Serve in a bowl and chopped parsley as garnish

Notes:

Can be prepared with spaghetti as a first course, a true classic of Neapolitan cuisine called "Vermicelli con Sugo di Polpi Affogati."

Leftover sauce can be enjoyed as a soup, topped with a drizzle of extra virgin olive oil and toasted rustic Italian bread.

*You can use frozen octopus, which is cleaned beforehand and tends to be more tender than fresh octopus.

Seafood Risotto
Risotto alla Pescatore ('risott 'do pescator)

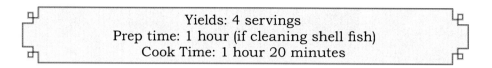

Yields: 4 servings
Prep time: 1 hour (if cleaning shell fish)
Cook Time: 1 hour 20 minutes

Seafood risotto is a classic first course Neapolitan dish, with each region preparing its own variation with the catch of the day. There are a few things to consider when making this delicacy. First, it is essential to use a good rice, preferably arborio. Traditionally, risotto is prepared with fish stock made from various fish heads and shrimp shells along with carrots, celery, onions and sometimes tomatoes. This is a typical dish in Naples, a city that lives on the riches of the Mediterranean. It will intoxicate your senses and brings the true taste of the sea to the table!

The first step to preparing this amazing dish is to clean the fish. In our recipe we use fresh clams, muscles, calamari, prawns, squid and homemade fish broth combined with the freshness of various ingredients to make this dish a success.

Ingredients:

- 1 pound fresh cherrystone clams
- 1 pound fresh mussels
- 1 ½ pounds calamari (squid)
- 1 pound jumbo shrimp, shelled and deveined (save shells for stock)*
- 4 ounces carrot
- ½ pound onion
- 1 stalk celery

- 1 ounce fresh parsley, 1 sprig set aside for stock, the rest chopped and divided
- ¼ teaspoon salt, plus more to taste
- 6 tablespoons extra virgin olive oil
- 3 garlic cloves, peeled
- Pinch crushed red pepper
- 2 pounds plum tomatoes (abut 8), diced
- 1 cup fresh tomato sauce
- 2 cups Arborio rice

Directions:

To prepare shellfish:

1. Soak clams in a bowl with cold water and a pinch of salt for 30 minutes to an hour before cooking. When ready to cook, lift each clam from the water and scrub it to remove any particle or grit from the surface.
2. Place mussels in a large bowl and rinse under running water. With the back of a knife blade, remove barnacles and pull the beard out. Use a stiff brush to vigorously rub the mussels under running water to remove any dirt. Remove one-by-one from the water and set aside.
3. Gently peel the outer shell off the shrimp, then remove the tail. Save shell and tail for stock. Using a deveining knife or a paring knife, create a thin slit down the back side of the shrimp and pull out the black digestive tract, if visible. Do the same on the other side. Rinse the shrimp and wash them thoroughly with cold water. Remove and discard any shrimp that appear slimy, discolored, or which smell overly fishy. Set aside.

To Prepare calamari (Squid):

4. Rinse squid and gently detach the head from the body by holding the squid tail in one hand and the head in the other. Remove the cartilage from inside the body and the clear quill by gently pulling it out. Wash thoroughly and peel away the purple membrane from its outside. Using a sharp knife, cut off the fins. Place a knife just underneath the eyes and cut straight down to remove the tentacles. Discard eyes and beak (a bony piece of inedible cartilage). Pat dry before cutting. Set aside.

For stock:

5. In a saucepan, add shrimp shells, carrot, onion, celery, parsley, salt, and 2 quarts of water. Bring to boil. Skim foam as it forms and simmer for 30 minutes. Strain and discard solids. Set aside, but keep warm.

For Sauce:

6. Heat oil in a 3 quart pot. Add garlic and crushed red pepper and sauté until garlic is golden brown. Add tomatoes and simmer for 10 minutes. Add tomato sauce and half of the parsley. Cook 5 minutes. Add calamari and cook 15 to 20 minutes until tender.

To finish:

7. In a 2 quart heavy-bottomed pot warm olive oil. Add rice and sauté for a few minutes. Slowly add shrimp stock, little by little, while continually stirring. When rice is cooked halfway, about 15 to 20 minutes, add mussels, clams, shrimp, tomato sauce with calamari and the remaining parsley. Mix well and cook covered on a low flame for 5 to 10 minutes. Season to taste and serve.

Notes:

You can use any frozen shellfish you prefer but the taste will be slightly different. Use whole frozen shrimp. Do not defrost shrimp completely. Peel and proceed as you would with fresh shrimp, without rinsing them.

Vegetables

"Le Verdure"

Vegetables play a large part in the Campania region, which is known as one of the most productive regions traditionally devoted to intense cultivation, especially of vegetables. The fertile soil provides the landscape where an abundance of fresh vegetables including tomatoes, salad greens, garlic, peppers, eggplants and herbs can grow. My family has developed an almost infinite number of vegetable recipes that have been passed down from generation to generation. Some of these recipes include different methods of preserving vegetables, since refrigeration did not exist years ago and only seasonal vegetables were used. Many vegetables were preserved in olive oil, vinegar, or turned into marmalades, without the use of preservatives and synthetic additives. Only spices such as wild herbs and garlic were added. These traditions are still carried out in our family today and considered real delicacies amongst family and friends!

These are some of our favorite, traditional vegetable side dishes that can also be enjoyed as a main meal.

Friggitelli Peppers with Tomatoes (Friggitelli al Pomodoro) 74

Grilled Artichokes (Carciofi Grigliati) 76

Scapece Style Zucchini (Zucchini Alla Scapece) 78

Friggitelli Peppers with Tomatoes
Friggitelli al Pomodoro -('E paparuncill c'a pummarole)

Yields: 4 servings
Prep Time: 10 minutes
Cooking Time: 40 minutes

"*Friggitelli*" is a type of pepper common in southern Italy and known in Naples as "*puparuncielli*," small green peppers with elongated shape that are typically sweet - except for the occasional spicy surprise! It was given the name friggitelli because they were traditionally fried in a pan with olive oil and without breading. Friggitelli are used in various recipes such as a pizza topping, in sandwiches, or in omelettes. In the United States they are similar to shishito peppers.

This recipe is simple and quick to prepare and one that we consider a specialty; a tasty dish with intense flavors, making it a perfect side dish that is delicious both hot and cold.

Ingredients:

- 1 pound shishito peppers (friggitelli) cleaned, stem removed, and patted dry
- 4 tablespoon extra virgin olive oil, divided
- 1 teaspoon sea salt, divided
- ¼ cup extra virgin olive oil
- 2 garlic cloves, whole
- 4 plum tomatoes, chopped
- Pinch of fresh oregano
- Pinch of crushed red pepper
- 5 to 6 fresh basil leaves, whole

Directions:

1. Preheat oven to 400°F.
2. Line a baking sheet with parchment paper. In a large bowl mix together peppers, 1 tablespoon of olive oil, and ½ teaspoon of salt and toss the peppers until evenly coated. Transfer peppers to prepared baking sheet and roast in the oven for 15 to 20 minutes, turning peppers halfway through, until peppers are soft and golden brown. Remove from oven and set aside.
3. Heat 3 tablespoons of oil in a large high-sided sauté pan. Add garlic and sauté until garlic turns a golden brown, then add tomatoes, oregano, and pepper and cook for 5 minutes. Add roasted peppers, fresh basil, and cook for 8 to 10 minutes. Gently mix well and add salt to taste.
4. Place on a serving platter and garnish with fresh basil leaves.

Notes:

Use as a side dish, paired with meat and fish. Or serve as an appetizer with crostini.

An alternative is to stuff friggitelli with your preferred filling - our favorite is with ground beef, eggs, parsley, minced garlic, grated bread, and various cheeses such as mozzarella, smoked scamorza, Parmigiano Reggiano, or pecorino Romano. Bake for 20 minutes at 350°F.

Grilled Artichokes
Carciofi Grigliati ('E carcioffole arrustute)

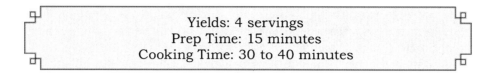

Yields: 4 servings
Prep Time: 15 minutes
Cooking Time: 30 to 40 minutes

"*Carciofi grigliati,*" in season from October to March, are a typical dish of the Campania traditions that have become a ritual for the Neapolitan table. These vegetables are a goodness that you find everywhere in Naples, predominantly during peak time. Traditionally they were cooked on hot coals covered with wet straw paper giving these grilled artichokes a truly extraordinary taste. They are a favorite, impressive and delicious side dish. Grilled artichokes are substantial and tasty and perfect for our vegetarians friends. Artichokes can be made into a main meal by adding them to tomatoes or a green salad. The following is a simple recipe that is suitable for different occasions, full of flavor and are delectable both hot and cold.

Ingredients:

- 2 lemons, halved crosswise, plus juice
- 4 large globe artichokes, washed
- ½ teaspoon salt
- 2 garlic cloves, minced
- 2 sprigs of fresh parsley, minced
- ½ cup extra virgin olive oil, plus more for oiling cast iron grill
- 2 teaspoons balsamic vinegar
- Pinch of sea salt
- Pinch of ground black pepper

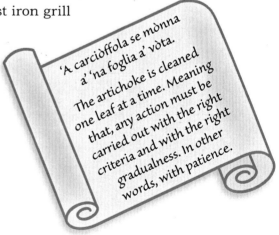

'A carciòffola se mònna a' 'na foglia a' vòta.
The artichoke is cleaned one leaf at a time. Meaning that, any action must be carried out with the right criteria and with the right gradualness. In other words, with patience.

Directions:

To prep the artichokes:

1. Prepare a large bowl with fresh water, juice of 1 lemon and spent lemon halves.
2. To prepare the artichokes: Remove the outermost hard leaves of the artichokes using a serrated knife or kitchen shears and cut off and discard the top 1/3 of the artichokes. Use scissors to snip away the pointy tips of the artichoke leaves. Using a paring knife or vegetable peeler, cut away the thick outer layer of the artichoke stems. Trim the stems 1½ to 2 inches from the base of the artichoke. Cut the artichokes in half lengthwise and using a strong metal spoon, scoop out the fuzzy chokes and the small inner artichoke leaves. Rub artichokes with cut lemons to prevent oxidation and discoloration and place in the prepared bowl with water and lemon juice.
3. To steam the artichokes: Set a steamer basket in a large pot and add enough water so that it reaches just below the steamer basket. Add salt and bring water to a boil. Place artichoke halves, cut side down, in the steam basket. Cover and steam for 15 to 20 minutes, or until fork tender. Cooking time depends on the size of the artichokes.
4. Meanwhile, prepare the dressing. In a bowl mix together garlic, parsley, olive oil, and balsamic vinegar. Set aside.
5. Transfer artichokes to a baking sheet lined with paper towels, cut side up, and sprinkle with salt and pepper.
6. Heat a lightly greased stove top cast iron grill on a low to medium flame. Using a pastry brush, brush the bottom of the grill with prepared dressing and place artichokes, cut-side down, and grill until lightly charred on one side, about 5 to 8 minutes. Turn over artichokes and continue grilling for another 5 minutes.
7. Arrange grilled artichokes on a serving platter and season with the dressing. Garnish with chopped parsley.

Notes:

Artichokes can also be grilled on a barbecue. Preheat grill to a medium heat. Brush artichokes with dressing and lightly season with salt and pepper. Follow step number 6 for grilling.

Store leftover artichokes in an airtight container refrigerated for three days. Leave at room temperature for 30 minutes before serving.

Scapece Style Zucchini
Zucchini Alla Scapece (Cucuzziell a scapece)

Yields: 3 to 4 servings
Prep Time: 10 minutes, plus time to dehydrate
Cook Time: 15 minutes

One of the tastiest and favorite summer time Neapolitan side dishes that exists! Vinegar was once an ancient way of preserving foods and it is now part of the culinary arts with *"scapece"* referring to the process of marinating with vinegar.

In Italy extra virgin olive oil is known as liquid gold and these zucchini are our small golden coins. This flavorful recipe is all about zucchini, vinegar, garlic and mint. We love garlic and add more than is required in this recipe! The end result is a crispy, fresh, delicious and nutritious dish. It is typically served as a wonderful side dish but we also use it as an antipasto on crostini or to make a delicious sandwich.

Ingredients:

- 4 zucchini (2 ½-3 pounds), washed, patted dry, and thinly sliced to 1/8" thick rounds
- 1½ cups cold-pressed canola or vegetable oil for frying
- 2 to 3 garlic cloves, to taste, sliced
- 1 tablespoon chopped fresh mint leaves
- 2 tablespoons red wine vinegar
- ½ teaspoon sea salt, or to taste

*"Addò c'è gusto
nun ce sta perdenza.".*

*Where there is taste there is no loss.
"If someone likes to do something,
obstacles or impediments
will not be enough to stop them.*

Directions:

1. Line a baking sheet with paper towels or clean kitchen towel.
2. Transfer cut zucchini on the prepared baking sheet and cover with additional paper towels or kitchen towel and set aside at room temperature for a minimum of 6 hours or overnight to remove moisture.
3. Heat oil in a wide and deep high-sided skillet on medium heat. Fry zucchini slices in batches until golden brown. Transfer to a baking sheet lined with paper towels to absorb any excess oil.
4. Place zucchini in a large bowl and add garlic, mint, vinegar, and salt and gently mix together until well combined. Cover and refrigerate for 2 hours or overnight.
5. Place on a serving platter and garnish with fresh mint leaves.

Notes:

Store in an airtight container refrigerated for up to five days.

Alternately, roast zucchini in the oven at 400°F for 20-25 minutes and then broil for 3 to 5 minutes, or until zucchini is golden brown. Set aside to cool. Place zucchini in a bowl and mix with extra virgin olive oil, salt, mint, garlic, and vinegar.

Desserts and Snacks

"Dolci e Spuntini"

Welcome to Naples where desserts are of great importance and each has its own story. Neapolitan pastries are considered an art form, a vocation and an integral part of history and tradition. Each pastry, cake, cookie, with its own variation in taste and fillings, evokes memories, stories and special moments of life combining all of our senses - sight, smell, taste, and touch. Desserts, as well as Neapolitan rustic snacks, are true treasures that have been in existence for many centuries. I share with you some of my family favorites, but I can certainly create an entire book on Campania desserts and snacks alone. It was not an easy task converting these specialties to gluten-free alternatives but it was exciting and delightful!

Anise Taralli (Taralli al Finocchietto)..82

Easter Pie (Pastiera) 84

Ricotta Cheesecake (Torta alla Ricotta) 88

Walnut Cups (Coppette di Noci) 90

Anise Taralli
Taralli al Finocchietto ('E taralle c'o' finuchielle)
Also known as "Brennole"

> Yields: 35 taralli
> Prep Time: 2 hours 30 minutes
> Cooking Time: 30 to 40 minutes

There are those that believe that "*taralli*" were born during the 15th century and in the ovens of the poorest neighborhoods of 18th century Naples. In fact taralli, in all of its variations, is one of the most popular Italian snacks. My sister Lucia is a taralli expert, amongst others. As with all recipes in this book, it is one of memory. I followed her with pen and paper and wrote down approximate measurements and conversions. Through these interpretations we were able to recreate the recipe, after several attempts, into gluten-free deliciousness. For this particular recipe we added anise seeds.

Ingredients:

- ½ cup warm water
- 1½ teaspoons yeast
- Pinch of sugar
- ½ cup of white wine
- ½ cup of extra virgin olive oil or sunflower oil, plus more for oiling bowl
- 1 tablespoon anise seeds
- ½ teaspoon sea salt
- ½ teaspoon ground black pepper
- 1 large egg, beaten
- 4 cups gluten-free all-purpose baking flour, plus 2 tablespoons for dusting

> *"Addò mangiano duje, ponno mangià pure tre."*
>
> Where two people eat, there is also enough for a third. Meaning that, there is always enough food for everyone.

Directions:

1. In a medium-size bowl add yeast and sugar to warm water. Mix and cover with a kitchen towel. Set aside for 10 minutes.
2. In a large mixing bowl, add white wine, oil, anise seeds, salt, pepper, and egg. Mix together until well combined. Slowly add yeast mixture, then flour, and gently mix using a rubber spatula until dough becomes homogeneous.
3. When dough is ready, transfer to a floured work surface and knead for 5 minutes adding additional flour, if needed, until you have a soft round dough. Place dough in lightly oiled bowl, cover with a kitchen towel, and let rest in a warm part of the kitchen for two hours or until dough has doubled in size.
4. Line two baking sheets with parchment paper.
5. When dough is ready, roll onto a lightly floured surface and cut dough into 1 ounce pieces, then roll each piece into 6 to 8 inch strips. Dough can be shaped in various ways, our favorites being twisted rounds and pretzel shapes.*
6. Place shaped dough into two prepared baking sheets and set aside to rest for 15 minutes.
7. While dough rests, preheat oven to 375°F. Place one rack on bottom and one in the middle.
8. When dough is ready, place one baking sheet on the bottom rack and bake for 15 to 20 minutes or until they turn a light brown, then transfer baking sheet to the middle shelf and bake for another 15 to 20 minutes or until golden brown. Follow the same process for the second baking sheet.
9. Serve as a snack, accompanied by salumi and a cheese board or a nice glass of red wine.

Notes:

Gluten-free dough, for this recipe, is fragile and breaks easily. Use a light touch when rolling dough into strips and when folding to shape.

Easter Pie
Pastiera di Grano ('A pastier e' gran)

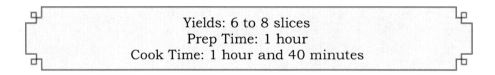

Yields: 6 to 8 slices
Prep Time: 1 hour
Cook Time: 1 hour and 40 minutes

A tradition that must be present for the Easter Sunday spread *"La Pastiera Napoletana"*! According to legend, la pastiera was created by the cloistered nuns of the San Gregorio Armeno convent around the 1600s, each ingredient signifying a strong symbolic meaning. The nuns would prepare *"Le Pastiere"* for the Neapolitan nobles and upper middle class. Tradition has it that the pastiera, a symbol of peace and the rebirth of humanity, is prepared on Holy Thursday and can be kept for at least 10 days.

Like any self-respecting regional dessert, it has its own variation and culinary secrets. These recipes that have been passed down from one family to another have a long preparation process that must be respected. Since we were little, my mamma has always prepared this classic rich and tasty version, one that she learned how to make in her early 20's from a family friend. She always prepares it a few days before Easter because in her own words, *"la pastiera deve riposare - avra' un sapore migliore"* (the pastiera needs to rest - it will taste even better). The filling is soft and creamy with a fresh and vivid scent of orange blossom. Mamma has always made it with *"grano"* (wheat) and to make this delectable dessert into a gluten-free alternative, changes were challenging since wheat is one of the main ingredients. Traditionally this pie was also made with lard, which gave it a greater taste. However, there is no wheat or lard in this gluten-free version but it is still incredibly *delizioso*! Additionally, we made our own citron with orange peel.

Ingredients:

For dough:

- ¾ cup white corn flour, plus more for rolling
- ¾ cup fine white rice flour
- 1 tablespoon vegetable shortening
- ¼ pound butter (1 stick), melted
- ¼ cup sugar
- 1 egg, lightly beaten
- 1 teaspoon vanilla extract
- 1 teaspoon baking powder
- ¼ cup ice-cold water

For orange citron

- 8 ounces orange peel (8 oranges), cut into strips, then cut strips to ¼" dice
- 1 cup sugar (or raw honey) mixed with 1 cup water

For filling:
- 8 eggs, separated
- 2 ½ cups sugar
- 2 cups ricotta cheese mixed with 1 teaspoon sugar
- 1 cup whole grain gluten-free flour
- ½ cup homemade orange citron (or use store-bought candied citrus)*
- 1 cup milk (or almond milk)
- 1 ½ teaspoons vanilla extract
- 1 tablespoon orange blossom water
- 1 teaspoon cinnamon
- Pinch of sea salt

For serving:
- 1 Tablespoon powdered sugar

Directions:

For dough:

1. Using a stand mixer fitted with a paddle attachment, mix together corn flour, rice flour, shortening, and butter. Mix to the consistency of breadcrumbs. Then add sugar, egg, vanilla, and baking powder. Mix to combine. Add water, a teaspoon at a time, until the mixture comes together to form a dough.
2. Shape dough into a ball, wrap in plastic, and place in the refrigerator for at least 2 hours or overnight.
3. Divide chilled dough into two equal pieces. Dust a clean working surface with corn flour and roll out one half of dough to fit the bottom and sides of a 9" springform baking pan. Press gently into pan and prick bottom with a fork. Refrigerate until ready to use.
4. Roll out second half of dough to a 10-inch square about ¼" thick. Using a fluted pastry cutter or knife cut into eight evenly sized strips. Set aside, refrigerated until ready to use.

For orange citron:

5. Place orange cubes in a 1 ½ quart pot with enough water to cover. Bring to a boil, then reduce heat and simmer for 35 to 40 minutes, or until peels are translucent.
6. Drain peels and add back to pot with sugar-water. Simmer together on medium-low heat stirring occasionally to prevent sticking. Cook until mixture becomes syrupy. Then remove from heat and allow peels and syrup to cool completely.

For the filling:

7. Preheat oven to 350°F.
8. In a stand mixer fitted with a whisk attachment beat egg whites until they form stiff peaks. Set aside.
9. In a stand mixer fitted with a whisk attachment beat egg yolks with sugar until light and fluffy, about 5 to 10 minutes.
10. In a separate bowl mix together ricotta and milk. Add to yolk-sugar mixture along with vanilla, orange blossom water, cinnamon, and salt. Fold in egg whites and citron and pour into dough-lined cake pan. Trim pastry from the edges of the pan and bake for 20 minutes.
11. Remove cake from oven and carefully place three strips of reserved dough across the top in one direction and the other three diagonally to create a diamond-shape lattice design. Return to oven and continue to bake for 40 minutes then cover cake loosely with foil and bake for an additional 30 minutes. The pastiera is done when the pastry is golden and amber-brown on top. A knife or toothpick inserted in the center should come out clean.
12. Cool completely before removing from pan. Ideally, serve the pastiera the next day. Dust with powdered sugar.

Notes:

The gluten-free pastiera can be kept for 4-5 days at room temperature, covered in a glass pie holder and in a cool and dry place, away from sunlight.

*Leftover orange citron can be easily stored in a glass jar in the refrigerator for up to two weeks. Try it added to other sweet recipes, in drinks, or on toasted bread.

Ricotta Cheesecake
Torta alla Ricotta ('A tort e' ricott)

Yields: 6 servings
Prep Time: 20 minutes
Cooking Time: 1 hour 30 minutes

This gluten-free ricotta cheesecake is a wonderful cake that will leave you speechless and will surely conquer your guests. This is a delicate, delicious and easy-to-make cake. A luscious cream is created by combining the unique and palatable flavors of lemon and orange zest mixed with fresh ricotta cheese. The ricotta gives this delicious cake a soft and creamy consistency that melts in your mouth at the first bite! Ricotta cheesecake is a special cake that is suitable for everyone and can be served at any time. It is one of those cakes that will be, without a doubt, one that you will bake often.

To prepare this cake use your favorite fresh ricotta, either from cow's milk or sheep's milk, brought to room temperature.

Ingredients:

- 6 eggs, at room temperature
- ¾ cup granulated sugar
- Zest and juice of ½ lemon
- Zest and juice of ½ orange
- 1½ pounds fresh ricotta cheese
- Powdered sugar for garnish

Directions:

1. Preheat oven to 350°F.
2. Grease a 9-inch springform cake pan with butter and dust with flour, or line pan completely with parchment paper.
3. Using a hand mixer*, beat eggs and sugar until light and frothy, about 10 minutes. Add lemon zest and juice, orange zest and juice, then add ricotta. Mix until well combined.
4. Pour mixture in prepared pan and bake for 1 hour and 30 minutes. The cake will rise during baking and lower once cooled. Turn oven off and keep cake in the oven for another 15 minutes.
5. Remove pan from oven and cool on a wire rack for two hours, then chill in the refrigerator for 3 to 4 hours or overnight before cutting.
6. Remove cake from pan and serve garnish with powdered sugar or with seasonal fresh berries.

Notes:

You can also add good quality dark chocolate, 75% or higher, melted and cooled to this basic version. Gently combine to the batter to have a soft ricotta and chocolate cake.

For an airy and lighter texture, separate the eggs and add yolk when the recipe calls for whole eggs. When all ingredients are combined, whisk egg whites to soft peaks and fold into the batter.

*Alternately, use a stand mixer fitted with a whisk attachment. Mix ricotta and sugar until smooth. Add eggs one at a time and beat well between each addition. Stop mixer and scrape down bottom and sides of bowl. Mix until all ingredients are well combined.

Walnut cups
Coppette di Noci (E coppette che noce)

> Yields: 24 cups
> Prep Time: 20 min, plus 15 minutes refrigeration
> Cook Time: 30 minutes

Walnut cups are a traditional dessert that are loved by everyone, especially my nephews! They are a treat that originated from Durazzano, a Province of Benevento, the birth town of my mamma and sister Lucia. This recipe is a keeper and has the double advantage of being excellent and easy to prepare. It is one that is typically shared during the Christmas holiday but it is excellent for any occasion. For this recipe, I used tin pans that my grandmother brought over from Italy. When I use them I think about how she held these in her hands and made the same recipes back in her own kitchen. *Priceless memories.*

Ingredients:

- 1 ¾ cups measure-for-measure gluten-free flour
- ¼ pound butter (1 stick) plus 4 tablespoons, divided
- 4 ounces cream cheese, diced
- ½ tablespoon ice water
- 2 medium eggs
- ¾ cups light brown sugar
- 1 teaspoon vanilla
- Pinch of sea salt
- 1 ¼ cups walnuts, chopped*
- Extra virgin olive oil for greasing
- Powdered sugar for garnish

Directions:

1. In a large bowl, add flour, 1 stick plus 1 tablespoon diced butter, cream cheese, and ice water and mix well with your hands, breaking down cream cheese and butter with fingers. Continue mixing and kneading until dough becomes homogeneous. Cover with plastic wrap and refrigerate for 15 minutes.
2. Preheat oven to 350°F.

For filling and finishing:

3. In a large bowl, whisk together eggs, brown sugar, vanilla, salt and 3 tablespoons melted butter, then add walnuts and mix together until well combined. Set aside.
4. Grease mini muffin pan with extra virgin olive oil. Scoop 1 ounce of dough using a cookie scoop and shape into a ball. Using your finger tips or a tart tamper, press dough into the bottom and up the sides of the prepared muffin pan. Add 1 tablespoon of the filling mixture into the muffin cups, but do not fill all the way to the top or the mixture will bubble over.
5. Bake for 25 to 30 minutes or until cups turn golden brown.
6. Cool and garnish with powdered sugar.

Notes:

*Substitute with nuts of your choice.

What is Gluten?

Gluten is a family of proteins found in grains such as wheat, barley and rye. Of the gluten-containing grains, wheat is by far the most common and makes up about 80 percent of the proteins in wheat. The gluten in wheat is called gliadin and is responsible for most of the adverse health effects of gluten. It is also responsible for the elastic texture in dough and plays a role in binding grain-based ingredients together in recipes.

The gluten-free diet is not designed for weight loss as many tend to believe. In fact, many gluten-free products may have the same or more calories than products with gluten. The gluten-free diet is beneficial when used as a strict, long-term plan for people with autoimmune diseases such as celiac disease, gluten sensitivity, or wheat allergy. For those with celiac disease, the most severe form of gluten intolerance, it is not a lifestyle choice but a necessity. Most people can tolerate gluten with no adverse effects. However, it can cause problems for those with medical conditions associated with gluten.

When following a gluten-free diet, the most important part is to look at the ingredients listed on a food label, usually located on the back or side of a package, when purchasing a product. Even if a packaged food product is labeled "gluten-free," be cautious of hidden food sources of gluten. Be aware of cross contamination by looking at the cautionary statements such as, "May Contain" or "Made on shared equipment, or in a facility that also processes wheat/gluten." Educate yourself about other ingredients that contain gluten as gluten is used in many processed foods and can often be found hidden in unsuspecting food products.

Having an intolerance or sensitivity to gluten doesn't mean avoiding your favorite foods. It simply means knowing how to avoid those problematic grains, which are hidden in many popular everyday foods. Fortunately, many foods are naturally gluten-free and there are plenty of gluten-free alternatives now available in supermarkets, health food stores and online. This ensures that gluten-free baking and cooking is not only possible but easy and delicious.

Gluten-Free Flours, Starches, Binders, & Leaveners

Wheat flour performs several different functions such as thickening, binding, changing texture, absorbing moisture and adding flavor to a recipe. Unfortunately, there is no single gluten-free alternative to wheat flour that can replicate all of these functions. Therefore, it is commonly suggested that you mix or use a combination of several flours and/or starches when making a substitute for wheat flour. Blending different flours is suggested, depending upon the recipe as there is no one ideal mixture for all recipes. Making adjustments to your recipe and doing a little experimentation is half the fun of gluten-free baking!

To preserve freshness, gluten-free flours should be kept in airtight containers and stored either in the refrigerator or freezer, as they tend to quickly lose moisture. All nut flavors such as almond and coconut should be refrigerated or frozen because they are more prone to rancidity due to their oils. All-purpose gluten-free flours should be kept in the refrigerator or frozen since they typically contain a combination of several nut or root based flours, which may be vulnerable to mold due to its high moisture content. Binders and leaveners should be stored in airtight containers and refrigerated.

Here is a list of gluten-free flours, starches, binders and leaveners that we use in the Culinary Genes kitchen. Some gluten-free flours have more nutrients than others and may require recipe adjustments or combinations.

Gluten-Free Flours & Starches

Almond Flour/Meal
Coarsely ground whole almonds make dark almond meal; raw blanched almonds, which means the skin has been removed, make light almond meal. Almond flour is finely ground blanched almonds and adds a subtly sweet nutty flavor, structure and crispness to recipes and almond flour is particularly good for baking cookies and for rustic cakes. May be used on its own or mixed with other gluten-free flours. Sift flour before using. Almonds are high in protein, calcium, vitamin E and healthy fat. A healthy alternative to traditional wheat flour.

Amaranth
Tiny, pale cream seeds that are milled into flour and have a nutty, earthy flavor and that tend to absorb flavors of other ingredients. It was considered a staple food in the Inca, Maya and Aztec civilizations. It is very nutritious, being high in fiber, calcium, folate, phytosterols and essential amino acids. Amaranth contributes to dense, brown crust in gluten-free breads. It is best when combined with other gluten-free flours, especially cookies, bread and pie crust recipes. The ratio should be one part amaranth flour to three parts of other gluten-free flours.

Arrowroot
Traditionally used as a thickener, arrowroot is made from a starchy substance extracted from the root of a South American tropical plant. It has a mild taste and provides structure, binding and liquid retention. Mix arrowroot with almond flour, coconut or tapioca flours for bread and dessert recipes. Today it is used interchangeably with cornstarch as a thickener, but with far less risk of the ingredients being genetically modified. Arrowroot also gives a glossy finish to sauces.

Brown Rice

Brown rice flour is made from the hulled rice grain and is considered a whole-grain flour, retaining all the germ and bran. Brown rice flour has a nutty flavor and is more nutritious than white rice flour. It is best when combined with other gluten-free flours for bread, cookies, and cake recipes. Brown rice flour is high in protein and fiber and is rich in iron, B-vitamins, magnesium and manganese.

Buckwheat

Although buckwheat contains the word "wheat," it is not a wheat grain and is in fact gluten-free. Buckwheat flour tends to be crumbly in nature and can be blended with other gluten-free flours to make bread. It is dark in color and provides a rich, earthy flavor. Buckwheat is a great source of B vitamins and fiber, is rich in minerals such as magnesium, iron and manganese and it is also high in antioxidants.

Cassava

Also known as yucca, it is made from the same root as tapioca flour. Cassava flour is grain-free and nut-free while also being low in calories, sugar, and fat. Similar to tapioca flour, it provides resistant starch, which has been shown in clinical studies to improve blood sugar levels and have digestive benefits. It has a neutral taste and texture, is easily digestible and is good choice for those with food allergies. It is similar to white flour and can be used as a 1:1 ratio in recipes calling for all-purpose flour or wheat flour and is best in recipes that don't need to rise. Cassava flour is rich in vitamin C, manganese, potassium, folate and magnesium.

Chestnut

A flour that is prevalent in certain regions of Italy, especially in Tuscany where it is a key ingredient for many traditional tuscan recipes. This flour is made with dry roasted chestnuts, is high in carbohydrates but low in protein. Mix chestnut flour with higher protein flours (bean flours) so that the dough holds together. Chestnut flour adds flavor, density, and heartiness to savory recipes such as tagliatelle, gnocchi and breads and is also great for making pastries, cookies, and pie crusts, as well as pancakes and waffles. It is a good source of B vitamins, vitamin E, potassium, phosphorus, and magnesium.

Cornmeal/Corn Flour/Maize

Cornmeal is a versatile pantry staple that is made from ground dried whole kernels of corn or maize, ranging in texture from fine to coarse. It can be either a creamy or a deep yellow color and stone-ground cornmeal provides added flavor and nutrition. It is a coarsely ground cornmeal that is typically used to make a crispy and crunchy coating for your food such as chicken, fish, polenta, or for baking scones, biscuits, cookies, and cakes. Corn flour is made by grinding the kernels of corn into a fine powder. Typically white corn (maize flour) is used for pasta, bread and cakes. Cornmeal blends well with other gluten-free flours and is rich in folate, thiamine, riboflavin, iron and niacin. Research has shown that cornmeal also has a high content of antioxidants. Store cornmeal in the refrigerator in an airtight container. Exposing cornmeal to humidity will make it go rancid.

Cornstarch

Cornstarch is made from the starchy endosperm of corn (maize) kernels. It is a common food ingredient, often used as a thickening agent in liquid-based foods such as sauces and soups. Cornstarch has a neutral flavor and no nutritional value and is used in large quantities for gluten-free baking adding smoothness and moisture to baked goods. Arrowroot or tapioca starch are good substitutes for cornstarch. Store cornstarch in a highly sealed container inside the pantry and away from sunlight and moisture.

Coconut

Coconut flour is made by drying and grinding coconut flesh. It has a light texture similar to that of regular flour with a mild coconut flavor. It is one of the most popular gluten-free flours around, rich in dietary fiber and healthy fats. Coconut flour also has a very low glycemic index. It is highly absorbent, meaning that it will remove moisture out of your baked goods, therefore we suggest adding additional moisture to give the product some structure. It is best if used with other flours and not on its own. It is also a good option for those with nut allergies.

Chickpea/Garbanzo

Chickpea flour is made from dry ground garbanzo beans (chickpeas), which are part of the legume family. It has a strong nutty flavor and a slightly grainy texture. Chickpea flour is a good source of fiber, iron and zinc. It is a plant-based protein and has heart health supportive nutrients such as magnesium and potassium. It is naturally dense and therefore works best in recipes that require structure such as bread baking.

Hemp

Hemp flour is a complete vegetable based protein that has an earthy flavor and is a deep, rich green color. Hemp flour is not one to be used on its own and is best when mixed with other gluten-free flours. It is perfect when baking, adding the benefit of hemp proteins and fiber content. Hemp flour is nutritious and rich in phytonutrients, vitamin E, carotene (precursor to vitamin A) and a number of minerals including magnesium, calcium and potassium. Hemp flour is a great choice for those who have nut and dairy allergies. Best to refrigerate after opening to ensure freshness.

Millet Seeds/Flour

Millets are a group of small-seeded grasses that look like tiny corn kernels. It has been an important crop and staple throughout Africa and was a main crop in China before rice was domesticated. Millet flour has a sweet, mild-tasting flavor and is a lovely creamy color, making it a great choice for sweet or savory baking. Perfect when blended with other flours adding structure to bread and flatbread recipes. It is high in essential amino acids, fiber and antioxidants, as well as being an excellent source of manganese, phosphorus and magnesium. Millet also naturally contains tryptophan, an amino acid that generates serotonin, which can help balance your mood, appetite, digestion, and sleep.

Oat

Oat flour is made by grinding oats and does not contain gluten as long as the oats used to make the flour are free from cross-contamination. While oats are naturally gluten-free, most are contaminated by wheat and barley. Therefore, look for the gluten-free label on the package. Oat flour is a delicious, nutty tasting flour that is high in dietary fiber, protein, B-vitamins, phosphorus, magnesium and contains various antioxidants. It also has a low glycemic index. Oat flour works well when blended with other gluten-free flours and is useful for building structure in baked goods. Baking with oat flour may leave your baked goods a little moist, therefore some ingredients will need to be adjusted to create light and fluffy end products. You can make oat flour by grinding your own oats in a food processor or coffee grinder.

Potato

Potato flour is made from whole peeled potatoes, which are cooked, dehydrated and ground. It attracts and holds water, which helps increase the moisture content in baked goods. Potato flour is ideal when combined with other flours and not used as the main flour in baking as it will absorb too much liquid and make the product gummy. It can be used to make everything from dinner rolls and sweet breads to pancakes and waffle recipes. Potato flour is a source of fiber, protein, vitamin C and vitamin B6. Potato flour should be stored in an air tight container refrigerated or in the freezer.

Potato Starch

Potato starch is made by extracting the starchy components of potatoes, then dried to a fine, white powder. Only the starchy portion of the potato is extracted and processed to produce a flavorless potato starch. Potato starch adds moistness to many baked goods giving them a soft texture and adds lightness and volume to breads. It is also used to thicken sauces, soups, and stews. It behaves differently than potato flour therefore it is not interchangeable. Tapioca starch and arrowroot are good substitutes for potato starch.

Quinoa

Quinoa flour is made by grinding quinoa seeds to a fine powder. It is a complete protein with essential amino acids that was once considered a staple food of the Incas, who considered it to be sacred. Quinoa flour has a slightly mild nutty flavor and is highly nutritious, packed with proteins, fiber, vitamins and minerals. Quinoa flour is easy to work with and is suitable for cakes, cookies and especially breads, due to its high protein content. The protein in quinoa flour gives structure to bread and will improve the overall texture.

Sorghum

Sorghum flour is made from an ancient grain that has been cultivated for more than 5,000 years. Is has a light color and texture with a nutty and sweet flavor. It is a great option for cookies and cakes and is best used in conjunction with other gluten-free flours. Sorghum flour is full of nutritious goodness, rich in protein, fiber, and antioxidants. This flour is often processed on shared equipment with wheat products, therefore look for a certified gluten-free label on the package.

Tapioca Flour/Starch

Tapioca flour is made from the tuberous roots of the cassava or yuca plant. Unlike potato, tapioca flour and tapioca starch are interchangeable with no discernible flavor. It has a fine texture and a bright white color and contains little nutritional value. Tapioca flour is often used as a thickening agent and provides structure, binding, and liquid retention. It works well when combined with other gluten-free flours for baking giving your final product an airy, chewy texture and a crispy crust.

Teff

Teff flour comes from the world's smallest cultivated grass seed and comes in a white, red or brown color. The light colors have a mild nutty flavor and the darker shades are more earthy in taste with a molasses-like flavor. It is highly nutritious, rich in calcium and protein and is the only ancient grain that contains vitamin C. Traditionally, it was used to make flatbread and it is best when combined with other whole-grain gluten-free fours providing structure in baked goods.

White Rice

White rice flour is made from finely milled rice grains that have been polished, removing all the bran and germ. It is neutral in flavor and is one of the most common substitutes for wheat flour. White rice flour works best when combined with other gluten-free flours for breads, pizza crust, cakes and cookies. White rice flour is a good source of magnesium, manganese, niacin, selenium, thiamin, and vitamin B6.

Gluten-Free Binders & Leaveners

Baking without gluten can be a challenge because gluten contributes important properties that help foods maintain their shape and holds the food together. In the absence of gluten's structural power, binders and leaveners become absolutely critical in creating the necessary binding, texture, elasticity and structure typically provided by gluten.

Here is a list of the binders and leaveners utilized in the Culinary Genes kitchen:

Baking Powder
Baking powder is a leavening agent that provides lift to baked goods. The active ingredients in baking powder is a combination of baking soda, an acid and a starch (to absorb moisture). Since the starch can either be gluten or gluten-free, it is important to purchase a baking powder with a certified gluten-free label.

Baking soda
Baking soda (bicarbonate of soda) is a leavening agent that provides a lift to baked goods and is used in countless recipes, including cakes, cookies, flatbreads, and more. It also helps improve browning and is typically used in combination with acidic ingredients for baking. Always mix baking soda with your dry ingredients first.

Powdered Psyllium Husk
Psyllium is a soluble fiber derived from the husks around the seeds of the psyllium plant, also known at the "*Plantago ovata.*" It is known as a bulk-forming laxative, meaning that it absorbs liquid and becomes a thick gel. When used in small quantities, it binds the ingredients together, mimicking some of the properties of gluten. We utilize powdered psyllium husk in place of xanthan and guar gum in recipes because it is our preferred binding agent. It has many beneficial health properties and is great for gluten-free baking. It enables bread to hold more moisture and achieve a light, airy consistency and helps make dough more pliable, making it easier to handle and shape or roll out.

Yeast
Active dry yeast is the original all-natural yeast that has been used for many centuries by bread bakers. It is used as a leavening agent and provides the ideal activity in all yeasted doughs. The main difference between commonly used yeasts is the moisture content. Active dry yeast must be dissolved in liquid before it is combined with other ingredients, whereas instant yeast (fast-acting yeast) can be added to dry ingredients.

Gluten -Free Flour Blends & Mixes

For convenience we have developed some of the recipes in this book using commercially made, premixed flour blends, as well as homemade flour mixes. Please keep in mind that because gluten-free flour does not behave the same way as wheat flour, a gluten-free mix may work well for one recipe but not for another.

Gluten-Free All Purpose Baking Flour

A commercially made blend that contains the following stone ground flours: garbanzo bean flour, potato starch, whole grain white sorghum flour, tapioca flour and fava bean flour. This blend is a great option for those with celiac disease or a gluten sensitivity. This gluten free flour blend can replace regular all-purpose flour in a variety of recipes. We also like this blend because it does not contain xanthan gum or guar gum, as we primarily use powdered psyllium husk as a binding agent.

This gluten-free all-purpose baking flour blend works well in recipes that call for baking powder or yeast and is ideal for many gluten-free recipes such as, pasta dough, pie crust, and pizza.

Use for the following recipes: *Fried Mini Pizzas, Twice Baked Bread with Beans, Escarole Pie, Anise Taralli*

Measure-for-Measure Gluten-Free Flour

A commercially made 1:1 flour blend that is gluten-free, dairy-free and Non-GMO. Simply substitute this flour for an easy and convenient swap for conventional flours. Ingredients are rice flour, whole grain brown rice flour, whole sorghum flour, tapioca starch, potato starch, cellulose, xanthan gum, and is fortified with iron, calcium, and vitamin B. This flour mix is best suited for non-yeasted recipes such as muffins, cookies, and cakes.

Use for the following recipe: *Walnut Cups*

Culinary Genes Gluten-Free Pasta Flour Mix

2 cups fine white rice flour

1 cup potato flour

½ cup fine corn meal

Use this flour mix for the following recipes: *Pasta and Faggioli; Baked Tagliatelle Bee's Nest*

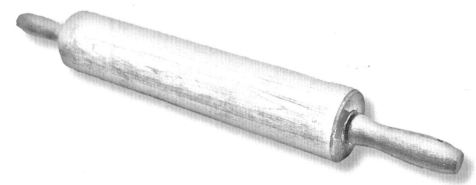

Glossary of Kitchen Utensils

Basket Steamer: A kitchen utensil commonly used to steam vegetables. It is a collapsible basket used to hold vegetables and other foods over boiling water so that they can be steam cooked.

Bench Scraper: True to its name, a bench scraper is used to scrape off the dough that's stuck to a work surface. It also is handy to use to cut the dough into portions with its edge.

Citrus Juicer: A kitchen tool that extracts juice from citrus fruits. It has a ribbed cone onto which a halved piece of citrus is pressed and holes on the top strain seeds and pulp while bottom cup collects juice.

Colander: A bowl-shaped kitchen utensil that is used to strain foods such as pasta or to rinse vegetables. The perforated nature of the colander allows liquid to drain through while retaining the solids inside.

Deep Fry Thermometer: A kitchen utensil used for testing the temperature of oils for deep frying and pan frying. Many have adjustable hooks or clips so it can be attached to a pan.

Devein Knife: A small sharp knife with a narrow tip used to remove the long black vein that runs down the length of a shrimp.

Dry Measuring Cups: Kitchen essentials for baked goods that come in graduated sizes and used to measure amounts of dry foods such as flour, sugar, nuts and berries. Dry ingredients should be spooned lightly into the measuring cup and then leveled off with the straight edge of a knife. For foods such as nuts and berries, the cups should be filled and leveled off with your fingers.

Dutch-oven: A handy thick-walled cast iron or enameled iron cooking pot with a tight-fitting lid so steam cannot readily escape. It is used for baking, roasting, braising and boiling, going from stove top to the oven without concern.

Fluted Pastry Cutter: A go-to tool ideal for making clean and precise cuts through dough and pastries with a decorative fluted edge. Perfect for pies, cookies, various pastas, and crackers.

Food Mill: A utensil for mashing or puréeing foods such as soups, sauces, or potatoes. The hand-turned paddle forces food through a strainer plate at the bottom, thereby removing skin, seeds and fiber. Typically, they come with interchangeable small, medium and large plates. Usually has feet or side handles to fit on the rim of a bowl or pot.

Food Processor: A versatile kitchen appliance that consists of a sturdy transparent plastic work bowl that sits on a motorized drive shaft. The lid has a feed tube through which food can be added. It can easily chop, dice, slice, shred, grind and purée most food, as well as knead dough. Many processors come with a standard set of attachments including an S-shaped chopping blade, plastic kneading blade, and several disks for slicing and shredding.

Frying Pan: A long-handled pan with relatively low, gently sloping sides that flare outwards so steam doesn't collect within the pan. Used for frying over high heat and comes in a variety of sizes, usually 8, 10 and 12 inches in diameter.

Immersion Blender: A handheld blender that is tall and narrow with a rotary blade at one end. It has variable speeds, is entirely portable and may be immersed into a pot of soup (or other mixture) to purée or chop contents.

Kitchen Scale: A kitchen device used to record the weight of ingredients and other foods and is important for consistent baking results. Available in analog and digital styles.

Kitchen shears: A culinary tool that is a specially-designed, sturdy scissor for the kitchen. They have many uses in the kitchen such as snipping herbs, opening food packages, or breaking down poultry or meat.

Ladles: The perfect kitchen utensils designed for measuring and portioning liquids. A ladle is a large spoon with a deep, round bowl used for measuring and portioning liquids.

Liquid Measuring Cups: Kitchen utensils that are usually made of glass or plastic and designed specifically for measuring liquids. They generally have a pour spout with measurements typically on the side of the cup.

Mandolin: A compact and hand-operated kitchen tool with various adjustable blades used for thin to thick slicing and for julienne and waffle cuts. The key benefits are speed and uniformity in slicing, shredding, and sometimes grating.

Manual Pasta Machine: A manual pasta machine comes with several attachments, usually one pair of smooth rollers and a dual-sided cutter. The smooth is for rolling out sheets of dough and a dual-sided cutter can make fettuccine or linguini, for example. There are many more accessories available for thin or thick shapes, or even ravioli.

Measuring Spoons: Essential kitchen utensils that are available in graduated sizes and materials. They are used to measure either liquid or dry food. Measuring spoons will allow you to quickly and accurately measure your ingredients.

Meat Mallet or Meat Tenderizer: A kitchen utensil used to flatten and tenderize meat. It comes in metal or wood and in a variety of sizes and shapes. Meat mallets are very useful tools in the kitchen and not just for meat. They can crush garlic or nuts, smash ice for cocktails, crack lobster or crab shells;,and roughly chop chocolate, to name a few.

Microplane: A versatile kitchen tool used for grating cheese, chocolate, ginger, garlic, citrus zest or anything hard that needs to be finely shaved.

Non-Stick Fry Pan: A pan that was traditionally used for low-fat cooking and is great for cooking foods that stick easily to non-coated surfaces, such as crepes, eggs and fish fillets. Use only with heat-resistant plastic utensils to avoid scratching the cook surface.

Paella Style Pan: A wide, round and shallow cooking vessel that has two handles and comes in multiple sizes. They are designed to perfectly cook rice dishes made with vegetables, meats and seafood. The paella pan can also be used for au gratin dishes.

Paring knife: A small, sharp, all-purpose knife with a pointed tip that is ideal for detail work such as peeling fruits and vegetables, de-veining a shrimp, removing seeds from peppers, or for cutting small garnishes.

Pastry Brush: Also known as a basting brush, is a kitchen utensil used for applying glazes, butter and oil on food, as well as brushing crumbs from cake layers. They can be made of nylon, natural, or silicone bristles. Natural bristle brushes are considered best because they are softer and hold more liquid.

Potato Ricer or Ricer: A kitchen utensil that resembles a large garlic press and used to process potatoes or other cooked starchy vegetables. It has two long handles, one with a perforated basket at the end and the other with a flat surface that fits into the basket. Foods are placed in the basket and the flat lever-operated plunger is pushed down into the food, forcing it out through numerous tiny holes in the bottom of the basket resulting in rice-like pieces.

Rubber Spatula: An essential, multi-purpose kitchen tool used to scrape contents of bowls and pans without scratching the surface. Also used for folding in egg foams or whipped cream, as well as stirring and blending batters.

Sauté Pan: A wide pan with a long handle on one side and edges that are gently curved and are a little higher than those of a frying pan. A 10-inch sauté pan is commonly used in a kitchen.

Sautoir: Similar to a sauté pan but typically a bit heavier with straight sides. It is commonly used for sauces and reductions and is a good pan to cook protein in because the flat, heavier bottom helps the cooking process. The sautoir comes in various sizes up to 14-inches, but are almost always 2 to 3 inches tall.

Scoops: A utensil resembling a spoon that is used for portioning soft solid foods. Scoops come in standard sizes and have a lever for mechanical release. The number on the scoop indicates the number of level scoopfuls per quart.

Serrated knife: Also known as a bread knife with a scalloped and toothlike edge making them ideal for cutting through foods with a hard exterior and softer interior such as cutting through bread. It can also be used for cutting fruits and vegetables like lemons, limes, and tomatoes.

Sieve or Strainer: Strains liquids, filtering out seeds or impurities. It also works well for sifting dry ingredients such as flour. It is designed with either a mesh formation or perforated holes.

Spatula: An essential and multipurpose kitchen utensil used for lifting, flipping, spreading, or mixing. Spatulas come in many different sizes and materials with silicone and rubber spatulas being the most popular, which are designed not to scratch pots or pans and the material does not melt even when they touch extremely hot surfaces.

Spider Strainer: A long-handed traditional Chinese skimmer in the form of a wide shallow wire mesh basket that resembles a spider's web. It is used to remove hot food from a liquid or skimming foam off when making broths.

Springform pan: A round cake pan with sides that can be removed from the base. These pans are designed primarily for use with delicate dishes that cannot be easily removed or flipped from the pan such as cheesecake, flourless chocolate cake, fruit tarts, or savory dishes. Recommended for recipes with thicker batters.

Stand Mixer: A versatile kitchen utensil that is used to beat, mix, or whip foods and have powerful motors that can handle heavy mixing jobs. Most stand mixers are equipped with an assortment of useful attachments that can include dough hooks, wire whisks, and flat, paddle-style beaters. Additionally, attachments can be purchased to juice fruits and vegetables, grind meats, cut pasta, and churn ice cream.

Stainless Steel Mixing Bowls: Lightweight and non-reactive deep bowls used for mixing ingredients. They are easy to handle, won't break and often come in sets that store perfectly. Mixing bowls are used for working dough, mixing dry ingredients, mixing salads, whipping eggs or cream, and much more.

Stockpot: A classic pot used in traditional kitchens that is taller than it is wide. It is a large, deep-sided pot for prepping stocks and simmering large quantities of liquids.

Tart shaper: A traditional tool used by pastry chefs that helps even out the pastry dough into the wells of a mini muffin pan or tart shell.

Tongs: A kitchen utensil with many uses. It is a scissor type tool that comes in many sizes and is used to pick up and handle foods, such as tossing salads, turning meats or vegetables, grabbing toast from the toaster, or tossing pasta, to name a few.

Wire Whisk: A kitchen utensil made of wire loops fastened to a long, narrow handle. Configurations and thickness of the loops vary depending on the type of whisk you use. Heavy whisks are straight, stiff, and have relatively few wires and are generally used for mixing, stirring, and beating. Balloon whisks have many flexible thin wires and are useful for introducing more air into a mixture such as whipping cream, egg whites, or meringue.

"A meglia mericina:
vino e campagna
e purpette e cucina."

The best medicine is:
homemade wine and
meatballs

Meaning that, it is
the simple things in
life that matter

Index

A

almond flour 93
amaranth flour 93
anise taralli 82
appetizers/antipasti: 3
    fried mini pizzas 4
    potato croquettes 6
    twice baked break with beans 8
arrowroot 93
artichokes, grilled 76

B

baked tagliatelle birds nests 48
baking powder 97
baking soda 97
beans:
    and pasta 36
    with bread 8
bell peppers, stuffed 44
bread with beans 8
broccoli rabe 62
brown rice flour 94
buckwheat flour 94

C

cannellini beans 8
capretto, cacio, ed uova 54
carciofi grigliati 76
cassava flour 94
casserole, potato 42
cauliflower 14
cheesecake, ricotta 88
chestnut flour 94
chickpea flour 95
coconut flour 95
cod salad 12
coppette di noci 90
cornmeal/corn flour 94
cornstarch 94
corn pizza, beans, and vegetable soup 20
costolette di mailae con patate e papaccelle 60
crocche' di patate napoletane 6
croquette 6

D

desserts/dolci e spuntini: 81
    anise taralli 82
    Easter pie 84
    ricotta cheesecake 88
    walnut cups 90

E

escarole pie 26
Easter pie 84

F

fish pesce: 65
    peppered mussels 66
    poached octopus 68
    seafood risotto 70
friarielli 62
fried mini pizzas 4
friggitelli:
    al Pomodoro 74
    peppers with tomatoes 74
friselle con fagioli 8
fritatta 30
frittata di maccheroni 30
from the oven/dal forno 41

G

garbanzo flour 95
gateau potato casserole 42
gattò di patate 42
genovese sauce 28
gluten 92
gluten-free:
    binders/leaveners 97
    flour blends and mixes 98
goat with peas, cacio and eggs 54
grilled artichokes 76

H

hemp flour 95

I

impepata di cozze 70

K

kitchen utensil glossary 99

L

lamb with potatoes 58
lentil soup 18
l'insalata:
    di Baccala' 12
    di Rinforzo 14

M

macaroni frittata 30
maize flour 94
mamma's anello al forno con patate 58
mamma's pepperoni imbottiti 44
meat dishes/le carne: 53
    based tomato sauce/ragú 32
    meatballs 56
millet seeds/flour 95
minestra maritata 22
mini pizzas 4
mussels 66

N

nests, tagliatelle 48

O

oat flour 95
octopus 68

P

panzerotti 6
papacelle 14
parmigiana di zucchine 46
parmigiano cheese grind 34
pasta: 25 (see also tagliatelle)
  macaroni fritatta 30
  and beans 36
  and genovese sauce 28
  pasta, potatoes, and provola 34
pasta, patate, e provola 34
pastiera di grano 84
peppered mussels 66
peppers:
  stuffed 44
  with tomatoes 74
pesto:
  arugola/rugola 31
pie:
  Easter 84
  escarole pie 26
pizza: 25
  escarole pie 26
  fried mini pizzas 4
pizza di scarola napoletana 26
pizza, fasul, e minestra 20
pizzelle fritte 4
poached octopus 68
polipetti affogati 70
polpette di mamma 56
pork with potatoes and papacelle 60
potato:
  croquette 6
  flour 95
  gateau (casserole) 42
  starch 96
psyllium husk powder 4, 26, 97, 98

Q

quinoa flour 96

R

ragu napoletano 32
reinforcement salad 14
ricotta cheesecake 88
risotto alla pescatore 70
risotto, seafood 70
roasted lamb with potatoes 58

S

salads/insalate: 11
  cod salad 12
  reinforcement salad 14
salsiccia e friarielli 62
sauces/sughi: 25
  genovese 28
  meat based tomato sauce/ragú 32
sausage and friarielli 62
scapece style zucchini 78
seafood risotto 70
smoked mozzarella (provola) 34
sorghum flour 96
soups/zuppe: 17
  corn, pizza, beans, and vegetable 20
  lentil 18
  wedding soup 22
stuffed bell peppers 44
sugo alla genovese 28

T

tagliatelle:
  e fagioli 34
  nidi di uccelli 48
  birds nests, baked 48
tapioca flour/starch 96
taralli al finocchietto 82
teff flour 96
tomato sauce, meat based 32
torta alla ricotta 88
twice baked bread with beans 8

V

vegetables/le verdure: 73
  friggitelli peppers with tomatoes 74
  grilled artichokes 776
  potato croquettes 6
  reinforcement salad 14
  scapece style zucchini 78
  zucchini parmigiana 46
vegetable soup 20

W

walnut cups 90
wedding soup 22
white rice flour 96

Y

yeast 97

Z

zucchini:
  parmigiana 46
  scapece style 78
zucchini alla scapece 78
zuppa di lenticchie 18

Made in United States
North Haven, CT
24 February 2023

33114424R10069